When Fitness Goes Tech

Navigating the World of Digital Fitness and Wearable Tracking Devices

Maja Dakić

Apress®

When Fitness Goes Tech: Navigating the World of Digital Fitness and Wearable Tracking Devices

Maja Dakić
Novi Sad, Serbia

ISBN-13 (pbk): 979-8-8688-2456-2
ISBN-13 (electronic): 979-8-8688-2457-9
https://doi.org/10.1007/979-8-8688-2457-9

Managing Director, Apress Media LLC: Welmoed Spahr
Acquisitions Editor: Miriam Haidara
Editorial Assistant: Marina Engler

Cover designed by eStudioCalamar

Distributed to the book trade worldwide by Springer Science+Business Media New York, 1 New York Plaza, New York, NY 10004. Phone 1-800-SPRINGER, fax (201) 348-4505, e-mail orders-ny@springer-sbm.com, or visit www.springeronline.com. Apress Media, LLC is a Delaware LLC and the sole member (owner) is Springer Science + Business Media Finance Inc (SSBM Finance Inc). SSBM Finance Inc is a **Delaware** corporation.

For information on translations, please e-mail booktranslations@springernature.com; for reprint, paperback, or audio rights, please e-mail bookpermissions@springernature.com.

Apress titles may be purchased in bulk for academic, corporate, or promotional use. eBook versions and licenses are also available for most titles. For more information, reference our Print and eBook Bulk Sales web page at http://www.apress.com/bulk-sales.

Any source code or other supplementary material referenced by the author in this book is available to readers on GitHub. For more detailed information, please visit https://www.apress.com/gp/services/source-code.

If disposing of this product, please recycle the paper

To my family and AnnArt, the love and light behind this work

Table of Contents

About the Author xi

About the Technical Reviewer xiii

Acknowledgments xv

Introduction xvii

Chapter 1: The Challenges and Opportunities of Digital Transformation in the Fitness Industry 1

1.1 Digitization in the Fitness Sector 1

1.2 Opportunities and Driving Factors of Digital Transformation in Fitness 2

Increased Health Consciousness 2

Shift in Consumer Habits 3

Technology Innovations 3

Global Reach 4

Hybrid Fitness Experience 4

Community-Driven Fitness 5

New Revenue Stream and Market Dynamics 5

AI Personalization 5

1.3 Challenges of Digital Transformation in Fitness 7

Technology Integration 7

Adoption Barriers 7

Data Privacy and Security Concerns 8

Business Model Disruption 8

Person(alization) Limitations 8

Technical and Operational Issues 9

Measurement and ROI Difficulties 9

1.4 Key Takeaways 11

Chapter 2: Tech Trends in the Fitness Sector 13

2.1 How Fitness Trends Evolved.. 13

2.2 Hybrid Tech Trends.. 16

Wearable Technology.. 16

Hybrid Fitness Platforms and Smart Gyms.. 17

Augmented and Virtual Reality (AR/VR) and Metaverse...................................... 19

Smart Fitness Equipment.. 22

Gamified Fitness... 24

Holistic Health... 24

2.3 Software Tech Trends... 25

AI-Powered Fitness Applications... 25

Biometric Tracking.. 28

Experience Economy... 29

Gym Management Software... 30

Workout NFTs and Web3.. 31

Live Streaming Classes.. 32

Staff and Client Apps... 33

2.4 Key Takeaways... 34

Chapter 3: How to Stay Ahead of the Curve.. 37

3.1 Why Is Staying Up to Date Highly Important in the Fitness Sector?.................... 37

3.2 How to Adapt to Changing Fitness Technology.. 40

If You Are a Fitness Professional.. 40

If You Are a Fitness Client and Enthusiast.. 42

3.3 Key Takeaways... 46

Chapter 4: For Fitness Entrepreneurs... 47

4.1 Gym Management System (GMS) – What Is It and How Does It Work.................. 50

Gym Management System – User Journeys.. 51

Limitations of Gym Management Software.. 54

4.2 Key Features of a Gym Management System and How to Choose One for Your Needs?...... 56

Staff and Member App... 56

Membership Management 57
Attendance and Access Control 57
Scheduling and Class Management 58
Billing and Payment Processing 59
CRM (Customer Relationship Management) 59
Reporting and Analytics 59
Staff and Payroll Management 60
Marketing and Engagement Tools 61
Inventory and Point of Sale (POS) 61
How to Choose the Best Gym Management System 61
Benefits of a GMS for Your Gym Growth 67
The Best Gym Management System Examples 68
4.3 Mobile Apps – Staff App vs. Client App 80
Staff App vs. Client App: What's the Difference? 80
Benefits of a Staff App for Your Business 85
Benefits of a Client App for Your Business 85
4.4 Personal Coaching 87
What Is Personal Training Software? 87
Benefits of PT software 88
The Best Apps for Personal Trainers 90
4.5 Examples of Gym Management System 95
Bonus – Best Ways to Monetize a Fitness App 98
4.6 Key Takeaways 102
Chapter 5: For Fitness Enthusiasts 105
5.1 Age of Online Fitness – What Fitness Lovers Want from Their Workout? 105
5.2 Tech Trends for Fitness Lovers 108
Wearable Technology and Fitness Trackers 109
Fitness Mobile/Web Apps 109
Virtual Workouts and On-Demand Classes 110
Smart Home Fitness Equipment 110
Virtual Reality (VR) and Augmented Reality (AR) Fitness 110

5.3 Software Fitness Solutions (Mobile Apps, Online Training, etc.).. 111
Fitness Mobile and Web Apps.. 112
Video-Based (On-Demand) Fitness Platforms 114
Live-Stream Classes/Virtual Group Workouts... 115
Personal and Online Coaching.. 115
Interactive and Smart Training Software 115
Augmented and Virtual Reality Fitness Software 116
Educational and Skill-Learning Fitness Software.. 116
Community-Driven Fitness Platforms.. 117
5.4 Hybrid Fitness Solutions (Wearables and Connected Devices).. 117
Wearable Technology.. 118
Smart Home-Gym Equipment and Connected Gym Machines 122
Smart Textiles (E-Textiles) 123
Bonus – Match a Device Type to Your Goals.. 124
5.5 List of the Most Popular Fitness Apps and Wearables 125
The Most Popular Fitness Apps 125
The Most Popular Wearable Fitness Trackers... 132
Quiz for Fitness Enthusiasts 138
5.6 Key Takeaways.. 142
Chapter 6: Use of AI in the Fitness Sector 145
6.1 Use of AI in the fitness sector 145
Challenges and Limitations of AI in Fitness.. 149
6.2 AI-Powered Fitness Studio Management... 152
6.3 AI Fitness Software Examples... 155
AI for Fitness Users 156
AI for Fitness Owners 158
6.4 Key Takeaways.. 160

Appendixes: What Does the Future Hold? **163**

Appendixes: All You Need in One Place **171**

Bibliography **185**

Index **189**

About the Author

Maja Dakić has logged more than 18 years in business writing, translation, and sales. She holds a Master of Arts in English from the University of Novi Sad, Serbia. Following her business writing years, Maja transitioned to the IT sector where she gained a unique perspective on the impact of technology on diverse industries, resulting in her first book *Mobile App Development for Businesses*.

In 2022, she founded the sports organization "AnnArt," where she works as a CEO and a chief coach. This experience helped her gain more insights into the fitness industry and dive deeper into the world of fitness technology. She's a regular contributor to publications (*Data Driven Investor, Medium, AnnArt Blog, etc.*) where she has more than 150 published articles covering a wide range of technical and related topics.

About the Technical Reviewer

Branislav Manojlović is a mobile application engineer with over eight years of experience in native mobile development, specializing in iOS technologies including Swift, UIKit, SwiftUI, and reactive programming with RxSwift and Combine. He also has professional experience in Android development using Kotlin and Flutter.

His expertise covers the entire software development lifecycle, including both software development and quality assurance in Agile environments. He has contributed to large-scale, production-grade applications and currently works at Vega IT, developing complex mobile solutions. Branislav holds advanced degrees from the University of Novi Sad, Serbia.

Acknowledgments

This book would not exist without the love, patience, and constant support of my family. To my children, **Dorotea and David Dakić** – I love you *to the Moon and back*! Thank you for reminding me every day that unconditional love is the foundation behind every meaningful creation. To my husband **Danijel**, whose encouragement gave me the wings to create and become more than I imagined – thank you for being my rock!

A huge thank-you to my home of inspiration – my **pole dance studio AnnArt** and our members who turn this space into a creative community. What began as passion and a real-life challenge gradually evolved into the idea behind this book. AnnArt is not only a cozy corner, but a vibrant space that inspired and cultivated every idea within these pages.

A special thank-you goes to my tech editor, **Branislav Manojlović**, for being a helping hand for both of my books. His support and technical insight were invaluable in shaping this book, just as they were in my previous work. Having someone you can rely on consistently makes a difference that goes far beyond pages and chapters.

Finally, I would like to thank **everyone who contributed** directly or indirectly through research, images, information, data, and reports. Each contribution helped shape this book into a reliable and meaningful source of knowledge. This work stands on many shoulders, and I am grateful for every one of them.

Introduction

When Fitness Goes Tech explores the opportunities and challenges of technology use in the fitness sector. It explains modern fitness technologies, considers their implications for fitness entrepreneurs and enthusiasts, and offers tech examples for your best fitness experience. This guide reveals the leading fitness mobile apps, connected gadgets, and modern tech solutions to help you achieve your goals, whether to improve your business operations or optimize your workout routine and enhance well-being.

This book is intended for both professionals working in the fitness industry as well as all fitness enthusiasts - technical background is not needed. Fitness professionals will learn how to keep pace with the evolving fitness technologies and gain valuable information on fitness tech solutions to help them automate and manage their day-to-day operations. Fitness enthusiasts will find out how to get the most out of the fitness tech tools for their needs and will enjoy discovering new workout apps and ways to stay active in any situation (remote or not).

The opening chapter introduces you to the fitness industry and its remarkable expansion trajectory, triggered by usage of technology. You will learn how fitness businesses thrive in a worldwide market with the help of technology, its economic impact and what experts predict about the growth of the fitness industry in the future.

The **fitness industry** covers a broad range of businesses and services that help people stay healthy and active. It includes gyms, fitness and health clubs, personal trainers, wellness centers, fitness gear manufacturers, digital fitness platforms, and fitness mobile applications.

The main goal of these businesses is to help users reach their fitness goals - from weight loss and muscle building to general well-being.

The past decade has brought significant growth to the fitness industry, primarily driven by **technology advancements**. During the pandemic period, artificial intelligence (AI) has become an important tool for modern fitness studios, mobile apps and online platforms crucial to fitness experiences, and advanced technologies necessary for athletes and sport clubs. This blend of fitness and technology has allowed users to track their progress and gain results faster and professionals to handle business operations efficiently (e.g., *administrative tasks like registrations, payments, etc., tracking members' performance*).

Fitness has become a lifestyle choice leading to a shift in users' wellness habits. Modern gear, personalized fitness training styles, and pleasant surroundings are just some of the things that have attracted new types of users to the fitness studios.

Since technological progress (*e.g., smartphones, wearables, etc.*) entered the fitness industry along with the increase of health consciousness, the fitness app industry has grown rapidly. The sports industry has also actively adopted wearable devices for their needs like preventing injuries, tracking athletes' health, and improving performance. These technologies that help in tailoring training programs are set to further transform the sports industry in the years ahead.

From an economic perspective, the global fitness club and Gym Management System (GMS) market size was valued at approximately US$0.384 billion in 2024 and is expected to reach US$0.98 billion by 2033, growing at a compound annual growth rate (CAGR) of about 10.92% during the forecast period. Figure 1 illustrates the growth trajectory of the fitness club and gym management software market, highlighting the expanding adoption of digital management solutions within the fitness industry.

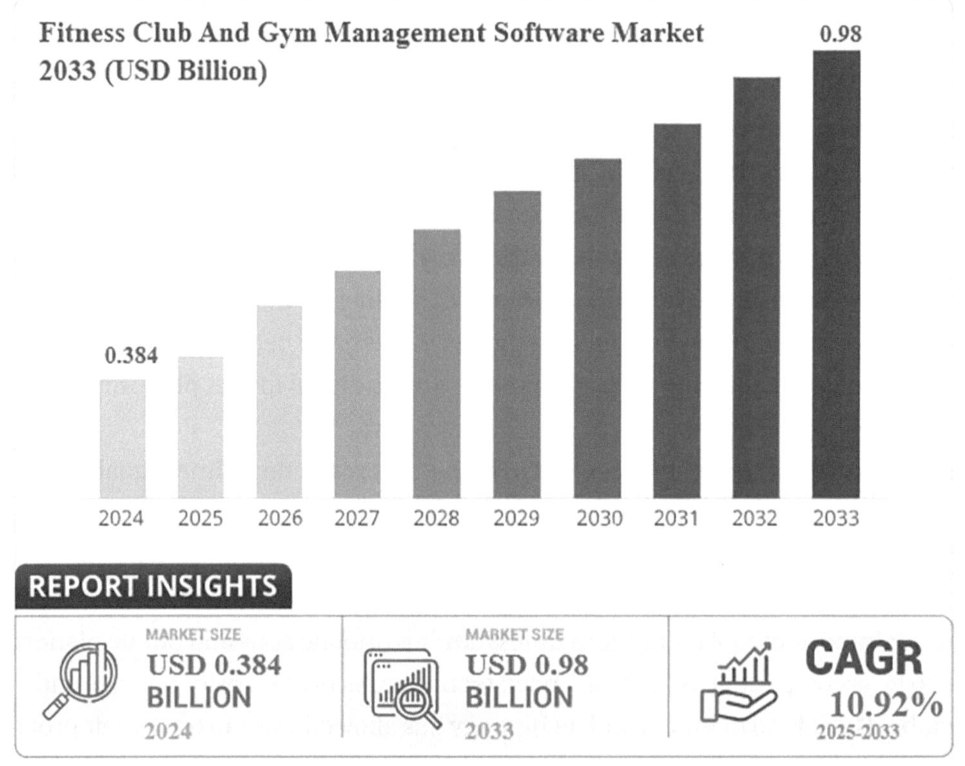

Figure 1. *Fitness club and Gym Management System market, Business Research Insights, 2025*

The sudden surge in CAGR was triggered by the increased demand during and after the global pandemic period. This was unparalleled since fitness clubs experienced much greater interest across all regions compared to the pre-pandemic period.

The digital fitness market is projected to grow at a compound annual growth rate (CAGR) of 33.5% by 2027. According to the Facts & Factors report, the global wearable technology market is predicted to grow to around US$251.32 billion by 2032 with a CAGR of around 14.80%. While wearables are leaders in the digital fitness market, fitness applications hold the second place with a total growth rate of 338.2% and a projected CAGR of 23.5% by 2028. Figure 2 illustrates the projected growth of the global wearable technology market between 2024 and 2032.

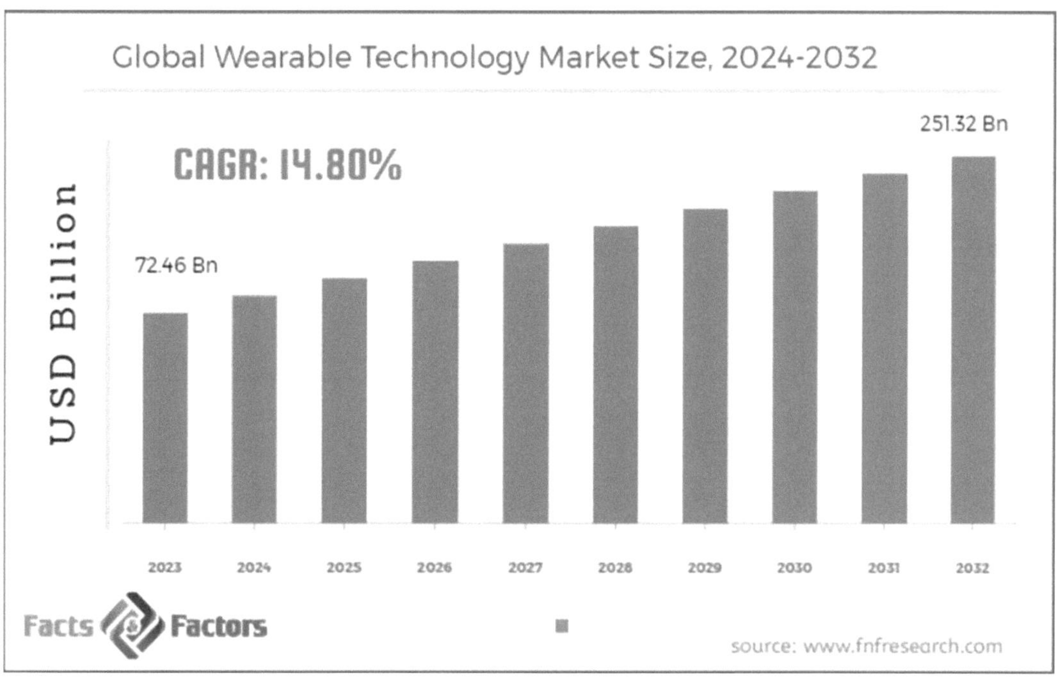

Figure 2. *Global wearable technology market size, Facts & Factors Report, July 2024, fnfresearch.com*

The key aspect driving the global fitness and Gym Management System market is the increased demand for digitized administration and personalized services. This market growth is further fueled by widespread adoption of digital tools (*e.g., wearables, mobile apps, etc.*) to help fitness clubs improve operational efficiency and fitness clients track their progress.

For example, Millennials and Gen Z are leading in demand for digital solutions and personalized experiences, with an impressive 79% placing a high priority on health and wellness. As shown in Figure 3, wellness priorities vary across generations in the United States. Generation Z ranks appearance among its top wellness concerns, whereas millennials place greater emphasis on mindfulness.

Gen Zers rank appearance among their top three wellness concerns, but mindfulness makes the cut for millennials.

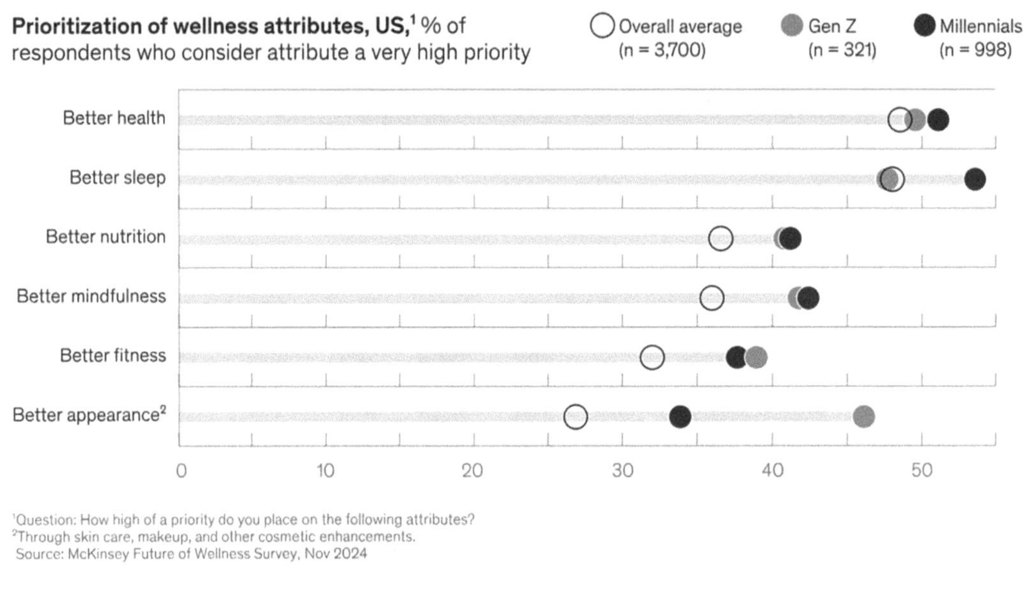

McKinsey & Company

Figure 3. *Prioritization of wellness attributes in the United States by different generations, McKinsey Future of Wellness Survey, November 2024, McKinsey & Company*

Social media platforms (*Instagram, TikTok, etc.*) have become the central spots for people to share milestones, leading to higher community engagement. Since demand for personalization increased, digital tools have enabled fitness clubs to offer tailored fitness plans to wider audiences. As many of us have busy schedules today, digital tools offer convenience to keep workouts on track and at our own pace.

Online fitness has now become a standard part of many fitness clubs – increased demand for health-focused programs, with emphasis on well-being and guided home workouts, was a trigger for fitness clubs to utilize digital tools further and offer educational content. This way, clubs keep their members informed and engaged on their fitness journey while additionally promoting services, and users gain workout plans tailored specifically to their preferences, availability, and goals.

Staying informed about fitness market trends is essential for both fitness professionals and enthusiasts as the fitness industry is projected to surpass US$200 billion in revenue by 2030!

Understanding the rapidly growing fitness industry and gaining insights into the market's trends and size will enable fitness clubs to make smart, strategic decisions and drive business success. Even a small shift toward digital will improve your business viability. For example, if you develop your fitness mobile app, you will be able to offer new products or personalized programs, promote your services, and educate your members – such an app can rank you higher on the market as being more appealing to modern consumers.

Following fitness tech trends will also enable fitness users to track their progress, train more efficiently, and gain results faster.

No matter if you are a fitness entrepreneur or just a passionate fitness enthusiast, there are plenty of opportunities for both to improve your business or facilitate adopting a more healthy and active lifestyle.

Whether you aim to boost member engagement or bring your workout to a new level for better results, this book will serve you as a practical roadmap to navigate the dynamic fitness landscape.

CHAPTER 1

The Challenges and Opportunities of Digital Transformation in the Fitness Industry

Chapter 1 reveals the opportunities and challenges in digital transformation of the fitness sector. You will better understand how the fitness industry grows with tech solutions (*wearables, mobile apps, data-driven training, etc.*) but also learn about the post-COVID impact and challenges of digitization in fitness.

1.1 Digitization in the Fitness Sector

Over the past decade the global wellness mindset has gradually shifted, transforming how people approach their health habits. Once focused solely on physical exercise, wellness today includes mental well-being, stress reduction, and daily activity as essential parts of a balanced lifestyle.

Adopting digital fitness habits was steady at first, but the pandemic period triggered a surge in digital adoption across the global fitness industry. Suddenly, fitness professionals had to shift quickly, from implementing online training to investing in virtual platforms and mobile apps. What was once considered a convenience unexpectedly became a necessity for fitness clubs to remain viable. As a result, digital solutions (*on-demand workout, virtual coaching, personalized programs, etc.*) have

M. Dakić, *When Fitness Goes Tech*, https://doi.org/10.1007/979-8-8688-2457-9_1

become permanent features in the fitness environment. Today's fitness landscape is based on **hybrid offerings**, meaning combining in-person experience with on-demand digital services.

The rise of wearable devices, fitness mobile apps, and connected equipment reshaped how people stay committed to their fitness goals. As people started to rely more on technology, fitness clubs started to invest in gym management software that supports both trainers and clients. These platforms help gyms streamline scheduling, bookings, billing, etc., while members benefit from personalized workout programs and performance insights that enhance the overall experience.

As digitization continues to transform the industry, fitness clubs that adopt technology will position themselves for long-term growth in a highly competitive market.

1.2 Opportunities and Driving Factors of Digital Transformation in Fitness

There are many factors that drive rapid evolution of digital transformation in the fitness industry. This transformation is driven by a blend of tech innovations, changing social habits, evolving consumer behavior, as well as broader economic trends.

Increased Health Consciousness

Growth in fitness and wellness services was fueled by a **rising awareness of health habits** across the population. People now recognize health benefits the regular exercise brings, not just for physical stamina but also mental well-being.

The pandemic played a key role in accelerating this shift. As a result of global lockdowns, demand for accessible health solutions skyrocketed, leading to the rapid **expansion of virtual fitness programs** and apps and home workout equipment.

Today's consumers seek wellness experiences that extend beyond traditional workouts. They expect services that support their entire health journey, from guided meditation and personalized nutrition plans to devices to improve sleep habits.

Fitness is no longer defined by physical activity only – today, it represents an **integrated approach to overall wellness**, including mental health (e.g., *stress reduction*), sleep quality, nutrition, and recovery.

Fitness professionals should align their offerings with holistic health trends and provide digital services to better meet clients' expectations and build long-term loyalty.

Shift in Consumer Habits

Customer expectations are one of the main drivers of digital adoption in the fitness industry. Since fitness clients now increasingly seek training on their terms, generic workout plans no longer meet the expectations.

Consumers' habits evolved demanding **personalization and convenience** and flexible fitness solutions that fit into their busy lives. Modern fitness audiences want programs tailored to their health status, fitness level, personal preferences, and specific goals (*heart rate [HR], sleep, nutrition, etc., tracking results, and getting feedback*). Integrating wearable technology, such as Apple Watch or Fitbit, can be a smart strategic move for fitness clubs. People no longer respond to flashy promises - they expect real, proven results.

For clubs, live-streaming workouts allow members to **train anytime and anywhere**, not disrupting their busy lifestyle. Integrating Artificial Intelligence (AI) and data to **personalize offers** will increase members' engagement and retention.

Finally, **data-driven strategy** is now the standard, with consumers expecting measurable outcomes and progress tracking through analytics and smart technology.

Technology Innovations

When technology entered the fitness industry, whole new horizons opened up.

Wearable devices, virtual training platforms, and **mobile apps** have significantly increased both consumers' engagement and operational efficiency for fitness clubs. Digital platforms can use biometric or performance data to tailor personalized training plans, where apps learn from user progress. Wearables and other **IoT (Internet of Things)** devices connect smart gym equipment and allow continuous data collection (*e.g., heart rate, steps, sleep quality*), while mobile apps enable remote workout and coaching anytime, from anywhere. These real-time health insights not only help users optimize their fitness routines but also provide gym owners with valuable data to make smarter decisions for boosting member engagement or adjusting training programs.

Artificial Intelligence (AI) further enhances this ecosystem, offering smart workout planning and adaptive coaching with personalized recommendations, helping fitness clubs and enthusiasts to create custom workout plans, predict results, and achieve results quicker. Meanwhile, integrating **virtual and augmented reality (VR and AR)** introduces interactive, game-like elements that make workouts more fun.

All these technological innovations give users deeper insight into their progress and empower fitness businesses to scale their operations and deliver immersive fitness experiences.

Global Reach

Technology adoption unlocked global reach for fitness clubs, enabling them to connect not only with their local communities but **with clients across the world**.

On-demand training and **remote coaching** help clubs deliver services and support 24/7 regardless of location. With AI-powered coaching and mobile apps, fitness professionals can offer personalized, high-quality experiences across regions while gamification features (*leaderboards, rewards, challenges, etc.*) boost engagement and help nurture loyal communities. This model enables clubs to offer convenience to modern users while maintaining strong levels of engagement.

By leveraging digital tools, fitness clubs are no longer limited by geography - they can expand their audience, diversify offerings, and **build a strong global brand**.

Hybrid Fitness Experience

Possibly the most significant opportunity in today's fitness industry is the rise of **hybrid fitness experience**. This flexible approach meets the demand of modern consumers, providing the best of both worlds - personalized online workouts tailored to their specific needs and in-person classes for live interaction and community support. It gives users the freedom to work out whenever and wherever it suits them, increasing client satisfaction and fostering retention.

By utilizing fitness apps, wearables, or smart gear, users can seamlessly **blend live and digital routines** for an immersive experience. For example, a user can join a cardio class at the gym, track performance via a smartwatch, and complete a personalized mobility session at home, all through one platform.

That is why today's consumers increasingly choose hybrid models - they offer flexibility without sacrificing results, helping them to stay consistent even when facing a busy schedule or travelling.

For fitness businesses, creating more adaptable services will cultivate engagement, keep your members coming back, and position you to embrace future innovations such as AI-driven personalization and virtual reality training.

Community-Driven Fitness

Modern fitness is much more than just a workout - it is a connected **community** with digital tools empowering trainers to build supportive networks around workout.

Features like **rewards, leaderboards, and points** can transform workouts into interactive experiences that motivate users - people thrive on support and recognition so personalized messages (*e.g., completing a challenge, celebrating milestones*) will deepen their loyalty. Social features like **comments, shares, and challenges** can make the entire fitness experience more enjoyable, while live classes, **gamified elements, and online communities** offer support and bring people together no matter the borders.

Influencer culture also plays an important role (*Instagram, TikTok, YouTube, etc.*) as they can set trends and share routines, transforming the fitness experience into a shared lifestyle movement. This can inspire other community members to get involved and participate while fitness clubs can harness benefits to drive organic growth.

Fitness continues to develop as increasingly personalized and data driven, yet its foundation remains rooted in human connection.

New Revenue Stream and Market Dynamics

The digital evolution in fitness offers revenue streams beyond traditional memberships.

On-demand workout, subscription training, and products like **e-books** and **workout plans** provide consistent and scalable income. Fitness clubs can also profit by **selling gear, supplements, or branded products** through apps - modern digital platforms make launching custom apps easier, enabling clubs to reach global audiences. The examples are Peloton and Apple Fitness+, the most prominent players in the digital fitness space, each offering a unique blend of technology, content, and community.

Even after the pandemic period, the fitness market proved resilient with strong demand for hybrid and personalized services. This growing demand opens significant opportunities for long-term profitability.

AI Personalization

Since Artificial Intelligence (AI) entered the fitness industry, it has propelled growth by making training more accessible and scalable.

Virtual AI coaches can deliver tailored training plans, adapt workouts in real time, and provide feedback, without ongoing costs or scheduling challenges. More advanced **AI features (*motion tracking*)** can help users maintain proper form during workouts, ensuring effective and safe performance. Even if training alone, AI tech can emulate a trainer, providing personalized experience fine-tuned for the user's specific goals.

For fitness clubs, AI opens a whole new world - digital platforms now keep users engaged with smart features like customized reminders, milestone celebrations, and progress insights. **AI-driven services** can boost user satisfaction while helping clubs serve broader audiences with data-based training plans. Do not worry, there are many tech providers offering "off-the-shelf" solutions that can help gyms offer AI services without building those on their own.

Gaining insights into consumer behavior with the help of technology will ensure your fitness club stays ahead of market trends but also unlock new growth opportunities in a rapidly evolving fitness industry. As shown in Figure 1-1, Artificial Intelligence (AI) and Wearables enable users to track workout performance in real time, providing data on activity levels, physiological metrics, and training progress.

Figure 1-1. *Tracking workout performance via AI and wearable devices by Freepik. Available at: freepik.com*

1.3 Challenges of Digital Transformation in Fitness

Digital transformation in the fitness industry poses important challenges that impact everyone involved, from gym owners and personal trainers to app developers and fitness consumers.

Let's take a closer look at the main challenges that come with this digital shift.

Technology Integration

Many fitness chains, depending on their operational systems and size, face challenges when trying to integrate new digital tools.

Legacy technologies sometimes create **compatibility issues** and can require costly upgrade packages. Implementing comprehensive digital solutions can demand significant **upfront investment** in equipment, licenses, etc., which may be challenging for smaller fitness clubs. Adding smart gear, wearables, or AR/VR requires further investments while developing custom apps can be expensive. Without smooth integration between platforms, such as wearables, fitness apps, and club management software, it will be impossible to unify fitness and data, limiting a club's ability to deliver a truly personalized experience.

Finally, even after investing in new tools, fitness employees need time to **adopt these technologies** effectively, adding to operational overhead.

Adoption Barriers

Not everyone in the fitness community is comfortable with technology. For example, older generations and those less familiar with technology may **resist using apps or wearable** devices, risking feelings of exclusion.

This rapid growth of fitness apps, wearables, and digital platforms led to an abundance of options to choose – it can sometimes cause confusion and **frustration with users**, even leading some of them to give up altogether. With thousands of classes and programs available, users may face **decision fatigue** or feel unsure where to start.

Fitness trainers can also lack skills or motivation to embrace digital class format, slowing the effective implementation of digital tools.

Resistance to change, specifically within older generations, can be addressed through targeted strategies (*e.g., in-person education and guidance from coaches, step-by-step tutorials, simplified onboarding*) to mitigate this challenge.

Data Privacy and Security Concerns

The risk of cyber threats continues to grow as digital technologies become more widespread.

Fitness platforms collect highly sensitive personal information like biometric data, health conditions, location, etc., all of which require rigorous protection. Without robust data protection, the fitness industry risks losing consumer trust and jeopardizing long-term growth. Complying with regulations such as GDPR (General Data Protection Regulation) or HIPAA (Health Insurance Portability and Accountability Act) also increases the cost and complexity of maintaining these security standards.

While gym management software streamlines operations, it also introduces significant risks by storing large volumes of data about staff, members, financial transactions, and more. Any breach or misuse can have serious consequences for both fitness businesses and their clients.

Building user trust is crucial for fitness clubs, as many consumers worry about how their health data is used or shared. Transparent privacy policies and strong cybersecurity measures are essential to reassure users and protect their information.

Business Model Disruption

The rise of low-cost digital fitness alternatives caused a significant **disruption within traditional gyms** and fitness clubs.

The digital fitness market has become increasingly crowded making it difficult for both *new players* to stand out or *established businesses* to maintain their market share. As a result, many gyms have started mirroring their digital competitors, which benefit from lower overhead costs and flexible subscription pricing.

Retention, however, remains a major challenge. Digital members often have higher churn rates due to lack of personal connection and commitment that in-person gym environments foster, making it harder to sustain long-term customer loyalty.

Person(alization) Limitations

Fitness clubs should not overstep with digitization; otherwise, they may risk losing the human motivation and community support many people rely on.

While AI coaching may offer convenience, these tools cannot replicate personal touch provided by real human interaction. This issue also raises concerns among fitness professionals about their job security leading to resistance towards digital adoption.

Even if the club relies on platforms with highly developed algorithms (e.g., *body type, health conditions, and preferences*), it can still feel impersonal, especially for users who like peer interactions or support.

Fitness professionals should also keep in mind that if users frequently juggle multiple digital tools (e.g., *for strength training and nutrition*), it may cause disrupted fitness journeys instead of exciting experiences.

Technical and Operational Issues

Digital fitness solutions depend heavily on stable Internet connections and compatible devices - technical issues like **app crashes, slow loading times, or unreliable Wi-Fi**, especially in rural or low-coverage areas, can frustrate users and affect a club's reputation. Users want platforms that work around the clock, so any downtime or outages bring a risk of losing engagement or causing cancellations.

Creating and maintaining engaging digital content is also resource intensive. Continual investment for video production, app updates, and fresh programming adds to ongoing operational challenges for fitness businesses.

Measurement and ROI Difficulties

Tracking return on investment (ROI) from technology upgrades can be hard since fitness goals are often personal and long term. Improved customer satisfaction or higher retention does not immediately translate into revenue gains.

Although fitness clubs obtain vast amounts of data at hand, many of them struggle to analyze and interpret the information successfully. Without clear insights, it may lead to "**data noise**," where more data does not (necessarily) mean smarter decisions.

Overcoming these challenges requires a strategic approach that balances technology with human elements essential for effective fitness experiences.

Check Table 1-1 for opportunities and challenges of digital transformation in the fitness industry.

Table 1-1. *Opportunities and challenges of digital transformation in the fitness industry. Source: Created by the author*

OPPORTUNITIES AND CHALLENGES OF DIGITAL TRANSFORMATION IN FITNESS

OPPORTUNITIES	CHALLENGES
INCREASED HEALTH CONSCIOUSNESS	TECHNOLOGY INTEGRATION
CHANGING CONSUMER EXPECTATIONS	USER EXPERIENCE AND ADOPTION BARRIERS
FITNESS TECHNOLOGY ADVANCEMENTS	DATA PRIVACY AND SECURITY CONCERNS
NEW REVENUE STREAM & MARKET DYNAMICS	BUSINESS MODEL DISRUPTION
HYBRID FITNESS EXPERIENCE	TECHNICAL AND OPERATIONAL ISSUES
AI PERSONALIZATION	PERSONALIZATION LIMITATIONS

To successfully navigate both the opportunities and challenges ahead, the digital fitness sector must develop a detailed digital transformation strategy. While more personalized, efficient, and accessible programs are now possible, it's essential to evaluate current market demand and resource availability.

Identifying clear short-term and long-term goals, particularly around cybersecurity and talent acquisition, will be key to overcoming obstacles. By addressing these factors thoughtfully, the digital fitness industry can become more resilient and better equipped to adapt to the future.

1.4 Key Takeaways

- The pandemic period triggered a rapid surge in digital adoption across the global fitness industry. As a result, digital solutions (*on-demand workout, virtual coaching, personalized programs, etc.*) have become permanent features in the fitness environment.
- The rise of wearable devices, fitness mobile apps, and connected equipment triggered people to rely more on technology; thus, fitness clubs started to invest in gym management software. Today's fitness landscape is based on **hybrid offerings**, meaning combining in-person experience with on-demand digital services.
- There are many factors that drive rapid evolution of digital transformation in the fitness industry starting from increased health consciousness and shifts in consumers' habits to implementing technology/AI tools and introducing hybrid fitness offerings. These factors opened new opportunities for fitness clubs to reach global audiences, open new revenue streams, and focus on community-driven fitness.
- Digital transformation in the fitness industry also brings challenges that impact everyone involved. These include technical or operational issues, like system integration, data privacy concerns, limited personalization, and disruption to traditional fitness models. Fitness club owners can face technology adoption barriers from both clients and staff along with difficulties measuring return on investment (ROI) on tech investments. Even when fitness professionals collect data through tech tools, they may struggle to interpret it effectively, leading to overwhelming "**data noise**."

CHAPTER 2

Tech Trends in the Fitness Sector

Chapter 2 brings the latest tech trends in the fitness industry, from hybrid solutions (*wearable devices*) to the software side (*workout mobile apps, data-driven fitness methodology, Artificial Intelligence*). You will read about the pros and cons of each trend and be able to understand which one can work the best for your fitness needs.

2.1 How Fitness Trends Evolved

The evolution of fitness shows an impressive journey from basic physical movement to today's technology-driven, personalized experiences.

The foundation years (**1940s-1960s**) of fitness started with simple calisthenics and basic gym gear with focus primarily on basic conditioning and usually linked to sports preparation or military training.

As of the **1970s**, fitness started a "home revolution" – as treadmills, stationary bicycles, etc. became increasingly affordable, consumers could work out from the comfort of their homes.

During the **1970s and 1980s**, the first fitness stars appeared – Jane Fonda and Arnold Schwarzenegger introduced aerobics and bodybuilding to the world. The 1980s marked a fitness revolution starting with Jane Fonda and her famous aerobic workout video tapes. These years transformed the way people approached exercise – the fitness craze was not just about staying active but also a cultural revolution fueled by the rise of aerobics and gyms becoming social hubs.

The following period from the **1990s to 2010s** brought diversity through various specialized fitness disciplines like

M. Dakić, *When Fitness Goes Tech*, https://doi.org/10.1007/979-8-8688-2457-9_2

- Pilates and yoga *(personalized programs for weight loss, conditioning, flexibility, etc.)*
- Modern dances *(jazz ballet, liquid, flow, poi, etc.)*
- Calisthenics - *a form of exercise that utilizes body weight for resistance training, no special equipment needed and can be modified for diverse fitness levels*
- Pole Dance - *a mix of gymnastics, acrobatics, calisthenics, and dance where you train the whole body*
- CrossFit - *a mix of gymnastics, weightlifting, and calisthenics, focusing on conquering obstacles and training the whole body*

During the **2010s**, fitness experienced its first digital integration steps. Wearable technology, such as fitness trackers, became widely popular, allowing users to monitor their activity and health in real time. The usage of online platforms and mobile apps rapidly increased as workouts became accessible anytime and anywhere. Social media played a key role in building strong fitness communities, connecting people worldwide. At the same time, boutique fitness studios appeared, focusing on specialized areas and offering personalized and more targeted workout experiences.

Since the **2020s**, the fitness industry has experienced digital expansion with a comprehensive approach, "Omnifitness," meaning blending traditional gym methods with digital technology.

Recently, trends tend to focus more on personalization and holistic health. By embracing these changes, fitness professionals can provide safe and effective training programs that will help fitness enthusiasts reach their fitness goals. Figure 2-1 displays major developments in the history of fitness, including the emergence of home fitness programs, wearable technologies, and AI-enabled fitness solutions.

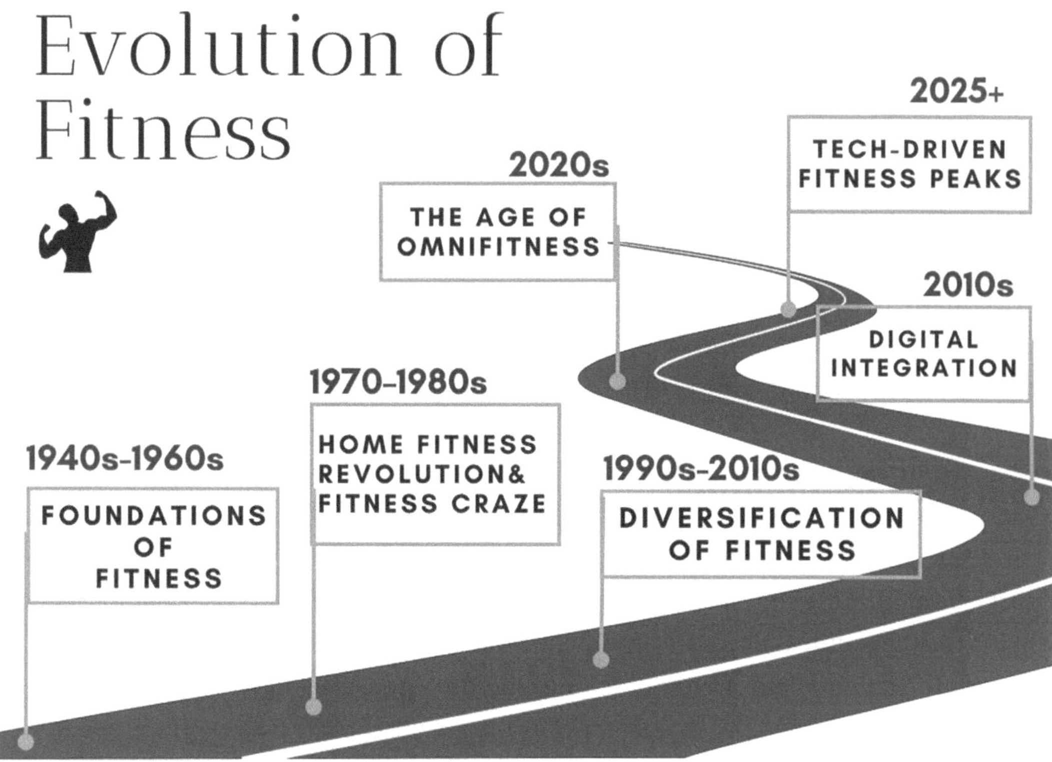

Figure 2-1. *Timeline of fitness evolution through years, highlighting key milestones. Source: Created by the author*

Technology became the leading driver of the modern fitness industry - wearable devices, mobile apps, and data-driven training rank among the top ten fitness trends for 2025, according to the American College of Sports Medicine's (ACSM) latest report in their *Health & Fitness Journal*. The report ranks wearable technology as the number one trend, followed by fitness mobile apps in second place and exercise for older generations in third. Mobile fitness apps have surged in popularity, climbing from the 20th place in 2023 to the 2nd in 2025.

Fitness has evolved over time, expanding from solely physical exercise to a more holistic service, now including mental wellness, recovery, and lifestyle habits. Despite digital transformation reshaping the fitness industry, there is still a strong focus on human interaction, social connection, and community. It reminds us that fitness is not just personal, but a shared experience. This evolution shows how fitness continually adapts to the shifts of social values, technology advancements, and a deeper understanding of human health.

Let's explore the most significant tech trends that will transform the fitness industry in the years ahead.

2.2 Hybrid Tech Trends

Hybrid technology has enabled gyms and fitness clubs to blend live and digital routines, creating more personalized experiences and driving remarkable user engagement. These hybrid solutions were widespread after the pandemic and continue to evolve, redefining how consumers experience fitness.

Wearable Technology

Wearable technology is the number one trend according to ACSM's health and fitness report - from tracking steps to monitoring heart rate and sleep patterns, wearables offer insights that help fitness users stay motivated and reach their fitness goals. Wearables also open the door to data-driven coaching where trainers can check client's metrics remotely, tailor the programs based on performance and progress data, and provide feedback.

Major brands like Apple, Fitbit, Garmin, and WHOOP already made a strong impact offering features like recovery tracking, VO_2 max estimates, and stress detection. More recent devices like smart shoes and biosensors go further with measuring muscle activation and movement efficiency.

Since AI becomes integrated more into wearables, fitness enthusiasts can benefit from more accurate feedback and recommendations. For gyms this can be a major opportunity as many wearables now sync with smart gym equipment.

Check some of the leading brands and their wearable devices in Table 2-1.

***Table 2-1.** Examples of wearable devices, their manufacturers, and key features. Source: Created by the author*

WEARABLE DEVICES AND MANUFACTURERS

BRAND	ECOSYSTEM INTEGRATION	FORM FACTOR	HEALTH METRICS	BEST FOR
APPLE	IOS, APPLE FITNESS+	SMARTWATCH	HEART RATE, ECG, BLOOD OXYGEN, SLEEP, SKIN TEMP	IPHONE USERS, GENERAL FITNESS
FITBIT	ANDROID, IOS, GOOGLE FIT	BAND / SMARTWATCH	HEART RATE, SLEEP, SPO2, STRESS, ECG	BEGINNERS, WELLNESS TRACKING
GARMIN	GARMIN CONNECT	SMARTWATCH	HEART RATE, VO2 MAX, HRV, SLEEP, RECOVERY, GPS	ATHLETES, RUNNERS, TRIATHLON
WHOOP	IOS, ANDROID	BAND (NO SCREEN)	HRV, SLEEP, RECOVERY, STRAIN, SKIN TEMP	RECOVERY & STRAIN TRACKING
SAMSUNG	ANDROID, SAMSUNG HEALTH	SMARTWATCH	HEART RATE, SPO2, ECG, SLEEP, STRESS	ANDROID USERS, CASUAL FITNESS
OURA	IOS, ANDROID	SMART RING	SLEEP, HRV, BODY TEMP, READINESS	SLEEP, RECOVERY, MINIMALISTS

Hybrid Fitness Platforms and Smart Gyms

Hybrid fitness platforms combine in-person training with digital tools for more convenience in today's busy lifestyles. As per International Data Corporation (IDC), 80% of fitness members expect digital features as part of their training plans, whether virtual classes, wearable devices, or on-demand workouts.

Leading fitness brands like Equinox+ combine luxury gym access with a digital app, while Peloton, Les Mills+, and others provide blended experience through integrated memberships. Barry's X also offers both versions with its signature High-Intensity Interval Training (HIIT) workouts, as shown in Table 2-2.

Table 2-2. *Examples of the leading hybrid fitness platforms and key features. Source: Created by the author*

HYBRID ONLINE PLATFORMS

PLATFORM	HYBRID MODEL	KEY FEATURES	TECH INTEGRATION	BEST FOR
PELOTON	AT HOME APP + IN-PERSON STUDIOS	LIVE-ON-DEMAND (CYCLING, STRENGTH, YOGA) LEADERBOARD	METRICS TRACKING, WEARABLES, BLUETOOTH	HOME USERS + BOUTIQUE STUDIO GOERS
APPLE FITNESS+	APP INTEGRATED WITH APPLE WATCH + GYM COMPATIBLE	PERSONALIZED WORKOUTS, MULTI DEVICE ACCESS`	APPLE WATCH SYNC, IPHONE, IPAD, APPLE TV, APPLE HEALTH	APPLE ECOSYSTEM USERS
LESS MILLS+	GLOBAL GYM CLASSES + STREAMING PLATFORM	BODYPUMP, GRIT, DANCE, STRENGTH & CARDIO PROGRAMS	APP-BASED TRACKING, WEARABLE SYNC	GYM MEMBERS + REMOTE USERS
EQUINOX+	LUXURY GYMS + PREMIUM DIGITAL APP	SOULCYCLE, HIIT, MEDITATION, YOGA	WEARABLE, APPLE HEALTH, PREMIUM STUDIO CONTENT	LUXURY FITNESS CLIENTS
BARRY'S X	BARRY'S STUDIOS + LIVE/ON-DEMAND VIRTUAL PLATFORM	SIGNATURE HIIT WORKOUTS, VIRTUAL COMMUNITY	REAL TIME COACHING, APP-BASED TRACKING	HIIT FANS & BARRY'S LOYALISTS
XPONENTIAL+	MULTI-BRAND GYMS + CENTRAL APP	10+ FITNESS BRANDS (E. G., RUMBLE, PURE BARRE)	APP SCHEDULING, FITNESS TRACKING, MULTI-DISCIPLINE STREAMING	VARIETY SEEKERS & BOUTIQUE STUDIO FANS

Some other examples include FitOn, **Myx Fitness, Tempo, Freeletics**, and more**.** All these platforms allow users to attend live and on-demand classes or book trainings via mobile apps.

Many popular fitness platforms, including **Strava**, **Fitbod**, **Peloton**, **Nike Training Club**, and **Myzone**, incorporate gamification into their user experience. These often feature real-time leaderboards, progress badges, and **social integration**, allowing users to compete with friends or broader communities, regardless of the location. Gamification also enhances **member retention and loyalty**, particularly when platforms tie achievements to rewards or recognition – it can bring a sense of fun and community to individual fitness journeys. This hybrid model supports a more convenient fitness journey, especially for consumers with frequent travel or schedule changes.

Biometric sync is another approach – wearables like fitness trackers and smartwatches allow users to adjust resistance or duration based on previous performance, heart rate, and fitness goals. This is a fully adaptive experience ensuring each workout is tailored to the user's needs on the specific day.

Smart mirrors and digital kiosks like Echelon Reflect bring interactive workout into both gyms and homes. These devices offer guided workout with real-time **visual and audio feedback**. In smart studios, these devices are used as self-guided hubs for users to select routines and track their performance.

As a fitness professional, if you integrate wearable tech or AI for more advanced personalization, you will be able to provide a smarter, safer, and more connected workout than ever before.

Augmented and Virtual Reality (AR/VR) and Metaverse

Augmented and virtual reality (AR/VR) and metaverse have introduced an exciting new twist to the way people experience fitness. As gyms continue to evolve, VR and AR technologies are enabling them to offer innovative fitness that is flexible, motivating, and inclusive.

The virtual reality (VR) and VR fitness games market is expected to grow to US$1042.8 million by 2030. With the use of VR headsets and sensors, fitness professionals can help users experience workout in totally different environments (*e.g., forest, city park, outdoors, etc.*).

Some VR companies offer multiplayer VR fitness games and activities for clubs, allowing them to train together in a friendly environment while in the virtual world.

Check the VR apps and features of the leading companies in Table 2-3.

Table 2-3. *Examples of VR fitness games and companies. Source: Created by the author*

VR FITNESS GAMES AND COMPANIES

COMPANY / APP	VR PLATFORM	WORKOUT TYPE	BEST FOR	KEY FEATURES
SUPERNATURAL (WITHIN)	META QUEST	CARDIO, YOGA, MEDITATION, STRENGTH	HOME USERS	REAL COACHES, LICENSED MUSIC, SCENIC ENVIRONMENTS
FITXR	META QUEST, PICO	HIIT, DANCE, BOXING, SCULPT	GROUP FITNESS LOVERS	MULTIPLAYER, DAILY CLASSES, PROGRESS TRACKING
ICAROS	ICAROS HARDWARE + VR	CORE TRAINING, BALANCE, FLIGHT SIMULATION	HOME & GYM INSTALLATIONS	VR-INTEGRATED EQUIPMENT, INTERACTIVE GAMES FOR FITNESS
HOLOFIT (HOLODIA)	META QUEST, HTC VIVE	ROWING, CYCLING, ELLIPTICAL (CARDIO MACHINES)	GYM EQUIPMENT USERS	SYNCS WITH MACHINES, ADVENTURE ENVIRONMENTS, GAMIFIED CARDIO
VZFIT (VIRZOOM)	META QUEST	CYCLING	BIKERS AND CARDIO ENTHUSIASTS	USES GOOGLE STREET VIEW, REAL-WORLD RIDE SIMULATION
LES MILLS BODYCOMBAT VR	META QUEST	MARTIAL ARTS CARDIO	HIIT/MARTIAL ARTS FANS	PUNCH/KICK COMBOS, REAL-TIME SCORING, GUIDED SESSIONS FROM LES MILLS TRAINERS

Platforms like **Supernatural**, **Les Mills Bodycombat VR**, and **Holofit** immerse users in gamified workouts that make fitness feel more like play. This approach is proven to improve both physical and psychological performance as studies show VR users experience **reduced pain perception**, stay in positions longer, and feel more motivated during strength exercises.

VR also unlocks the potential for **community-based hybrid training** as members can join live virtual classes from home or the gym, compete in shared challenges, and interact with digital avatars in multiplayer fitness settings. With **motion capture and real-time syncing**, users can compete, or receive coaching, even if they're in different locations.

On the other hand, augmented reality (AR) enhances the reality of fitness experience through visualization. With AR-enabled glasses or a smartphone, members can access gamified workout and coaching, real-time guidance, and visualized instructions.

Whether it's tracking reps or correcting posture, AR transforms traditional workouts into guided sessions. Some gyms are already using AR for interactive challenges, encouraging users to hit targets as part of their functional training, thus blending real movement with on-screen feedback.

Check some of the leading AR companies and their gamified apps in Table 2-4.

Table 2-4. *Examples of augmented reality (AR) fitness companies and apps. Source: Created by the author*

AR FITNESS GAMES AND COMPANIES

COMPANY / APP	AR PLATFORM	WORKOUT TYPE	BEST FOR
QUELL	WEARABLE + MOTION SENSORS	RESISTANCE-BASED WORKOUTS	COMBINES AR VISUALS WITH HAPTIC GEAR FOR COMBAT-STYLE WORKOUTS
POKÉMON GO (NIANTIC)	IOS, ANDROID	WALKING, EXPLORING	ENCOURAGES REAL-WORLD WALKING/EXPLORING WITH GAMIFIED AR CREATURE HUNTING
SKATRIX (BY REALITY GAMING GROUP)	MOBILE AR	SKATEBOARDING & TRICKS	USES PHONE'S CAMERA AND AR TO TEACH TRICKS, BALANCE, AND FORM
NEX PLAYGROUND (BY NEX)	SMART TV + AI CAMERA	FULL-BODY INTERACTIVE GAMES	USES COMPUTER VISION TO TRACK MOVEMENTS FOR FITNESS GAMES FOR ALL AGES
MAGIC LEAP X ADIDAS (CONCEPT)	MAGIC LEAP AR HEADSET	TRAINING, MOVEMENT-BASED	EXPERIMENTAL COLLABORATION COMBINING SMART WEARABLES AND INTERACTIVE AR DRILLS
MIRROR (LULULEMON) + FUTURE AR	SMART MIRROR (AR IN DEVELOPMENT)	STRENGTH, YOGA, BOXING	CURRENTLY VISUAL COACHING; FUTURE VERSIONS AIM TO INCLUDE AR OVERLAYS

VR and AR workouts will continue to transform the fitness industry – consider introducing some of these cutting-edge workouts into your club and grow your members' curiosity and engagement. Regardless of age, everyone will be eager to experience this "altered" sense of reality.

Smart Fitness Equipment

Smart gym equipment is rapidly transforming the fitness industry by enhancing both operational efficiency and user experience. These advanced machines offer real-time workout analysis - imagine a system that tracks users' performance and gives instant feedback on their technique. This kind of innovation can elevate the quality of exercise and significantly increase member retention.

Smart fitness equipment, from AI-powered machines to interactive cardio gear, is designed to optimize performance and maintain engagement. However, adoption may face resistance from some members. Training staff to guide users and clearly demonstrating the benefits are essential for ensuring client satisfaction.

The category has also expanded into smart workout apparel and portable gear that integrate biometric and muscle activity sensors. This smart gear connects to fitness apps to provide more detailed insights, like Hexoskin and Prana Wearable. Hexoskin makes smart shirts with sensors within the fabric, tracking important health data and users' physical performance. Prana Wearable is an innovative product which monitors controlled breathing exercises and posture.

Check out the list of smart gym equipment and gear in Table 2-5.

***Table 2-5.** Examples of smart fitness equipment and gear manufacturers. Source: Created by the author*

SMART FITNESS EQUIPMENT AND GEAR

COMPANY / APP	TYPE OF GEAR
PELOTON	BIKES, TREADMILLS, AND ROWERS WITH LIVE/ON-DEMAND CLASSES
NORDICTRACK (BY ICON HEALTH & FITNESS)	SMART TREADMILLS, BIKES, AND VAULT
ECHELON	SMART BIKES, ROWERS, AND TREADMILLS WITH LIVE CONTENT INTEGRATION
HEXOSKIN	SMART SHIRTS WITH ECG AND RESPIRATORY TRACKING
PRANA WEARABLE	MONITORS POSTURE AND BREATHING IN REAL TIME
ATHOS	SMART CLOTHING THAT MEASURES MUSCLE EFFORT DURING TRAINING

Brands like Peloton and Tonal offer interactive, instructor-led workouts with real-time tracking, while others like Tempo offer smart home gyms with 3D sensors, real-time feedback, and AI tracking.

Advanced home fitness gear now includes cameras, motion sensors, access to trainers, and more. The market now features modern equipment that bridges the gap between home and commercial gym experiences like Tonal offering electromagnetic resistance training with AI coaching; then **Speediance**, an AI smart gym for full-body workout and instant coaching; and **OxeFit**, an all-in-one fitness solution with 280+ exercises, real-time performance metrics, and interactive training options.

This new generation of equipment bridges the gap between home and commercial fitness, combining the convenience of personal training (PT) with the sophistication of professional gym technology. For fitness businesses, investing in smart fitness gear is a smart strategy as it will propel your business forward by providing a highly personalized experience for your users.

Gamified Fitness

Gamification is a rising trend that boosts user engagement by turning workouts into interactive, competitive experiences. Platforms like Zwift and Ergatta turn cardio or rowing sessions into competitive, game-like experiences, making workouts more interactive and motivating.

AI-powered home gyms are also gaining traction - systems like Speediance and OxeFit's XS1 offer adaptive resistance, hundreds of guided workouts, and real-time performance metrics. They're compact, intelligent, and designed to deliver full-body training with maximum convenience.

For fitness clubs, implementing **gamification** can be a strategic advantage since it taps into **human motivation**, **boosts engagement**, and increases **long-term client retention**.

Holistic Health

One of the most important trends shaping the fitness future is the integration of overall wellness into workout culture. Modern fitness users want more than just physical workout; they prioritize balance and long-term health goals. In response, modern fitness has embraced a holistic approach addressing mental well-being, recovery, stress management, and nutrition. Gyms and clubs are expanding their offer with breathing exercises, stress-reduction programs, and tailored nutrition support plans besides standard workouts.

Fitness wearables are the main drive of this shift - devices like Fitbit, Apple Watch, Oura Ring, etc., track not only activity but also sleep patterns, heart rate, stress levels and overall recovery. If users integrate it with a mobile app, they can obtain real-time feedback and personal wellness recommendations. Predictive analysis goes even further by detecting early signs of overtraining, burnout, or potential injuries thus helping users train smarter.

Wellness ecosystems are emerging increasingly - these are the platforms that link physical workout with recovery plan, nutrition tips, and mental wellness tools. Some popular examples include **Lululemon Studio** (*combines in-home, wellness focused digital workouts*) and **Xponential+** (*offers hybrid workout models from brands like Pure Barre/Cycle Bar while integrating recovery and health tracking*).

The wellness mindset is transforming fitness into a more personalized experience as the goals of fitness enthusiasts today are not just to burn calories, but to thrive physically and mentally. As the fitness industry continues to evolve, wellness goals (*health, balance, and recovery*) will be just as essential as strength or cardio exercise.

2.3 Software Tech Trends

In 2025, fitness software is increasingly defined by **personalization**, **AI-driven coaching**, and **connected platforms** that merge training, nutrition, recovery, and wearable data into a single cohesive experience.

The focus is shifting beyond traditional workouts, with **eSports** and **interactive gaming** blending entertainment with exercise to create more dynamic training environments.

Let's explore the leading **fitness tech trends of 2025**, and how these tools are reshaping experiences for consumers, trainers, and gyms worldwide.

AI-Powered Fitness Applications

"*AI algorithms have revolutionized personalized communication in fitness business management software and apps, creating highly customized and engaging experiences. AI learns from members' interactions and progress, analysing behaviours, preferences, and goals*," says ABC Fitness CEO Bill Davis in "How AI Is Transforming Fitness Apps" (Health & Fitness Association).

Artificial Intelligence (AI)-powered fitness apps redefine how people train, recover, and stay motivated, as these offer personalized experiences that adjust in real time.

AI-powered fitness apps can adapt variables like workout type, number of reps, duration, and difficulty level, helping users form sustainable habits and achieve lasting results. For fitness clubs, integrating AI-driven programs can create new engagement models, from **virtual training memberships** to **hybrid coaching services**.

Some examples of AI-powered apps include the following:

- Gymfitty and ArtiFit offer smart workouts adapting to user's needs in real time.
- Fitbod, Future, and Freeletics create adaptive workouts and offer personalized training plans.

- Tempo and OxeFit use AI to analyze camera/video input to correct posture or movement.
- Lumen and Zoe analyze users' metabolic data to provide smart meal planning and nutrition advice.

Other apps that use AI include virtual coaches, where AI voice and video coaches provide real-time feedback and recovery optimization where devices and apps suggest recovery strategy based on users' health level, sleep patterns, and more. With software analyzing biometrics, AI can offer predictive performance to suggest training volume, rest, and nutrition. Figure 2-2 illustrates the user interface of the Gymfitty AI-powered fitness application, which enables personalized and adaptive workout tracking.

Figure 2-2. *Gimfitty AI-powered app screen. Available at:* `www.gymfitty.com`

Check out the benefits that AI-powered fitness apps can bring to fitness users:

- **Smart Personalization** – Modern fitness apps adapt to users' performance, delivering real-time feedback and analyzing details like biometrics and preferences for tailored workout plans. Examples include Fitbod, Freeletics, Gymfitty, ArtiFit, Tempo, and more.

- **Virtual Coaches** - AI and video coaches provide guidance and technique correction and simulate a personal trainer without the additional costs.
- **Predictive Performance** - AI-driven systems analyze data like sleep patterns, Heart Rate Variability (HRV), or previous workout injuries to suggest the optimal training load, rest days, and nutrition plans.
- **Smart Nutrition and Recovery** - AI uses metabolic data to provide custom smart meal planning (e.g., Lumen, Zoe) and offer recovery tools based on elements like sleep, stress, or muscle strain (e.g., WHOOP, Oura app, Recover Athletics by Strava).
- **Workout Engagement** - Holistic tracking allows AI platforms to monitor workout consistency, suggest hybrid schedules, and improve user retention.
- **Genetic Integration** - DNA-based fitness planning includes personalized recommendations based on genetic predispositions like metabolism rate, muscle composition, and similar.

Social interaction is the strongest motivator in fitness and many modern fitness apps leverage it to boost engagement. Apps like Strava MyFitnessPal or Nike Training Club create a supportive community where users stay motivated, track progress, and celebrate milestones together.

Fitness and wellness apps enable not only fitness users but also trainers and clubs to scale their services, stay connected with members, and build new revenue via online coaching.

Fitness professionals may feel threatened by this piece of technology but while AI is powerful, it cannot replicate the **human element** that drives loyalty. Personal connections, group activities, and one-on-one interaction remain the ultimate retention tools. Successful businesses will combine **cutting-edge AI capabilities** with **genuine human connection** to deliver the best of both worlds - emphasize personalization, create fun activities for your users, and connect with them on a personal level - that's how to outclass Artificial Intelligence. As shown in Figure 2-3, the WHOOP recovery system integrates wearable sensor data with a mobile application to provide users with insights on sleep, strain, and recovery status.

Figure 2-3. *Whoop recovery app and wearable devices. Available at: whoop.com*

Biometric Tracking

Biohacking is rapidly gaining traction, especially among younger generations who are interested in using technology to improve their health and performance. At its core, biohacking combines **data-driven decision-making** and **cutting-edge tech** to optimize physical conditioning and overall well-being.

In fitness, this trend focuses on maximizing results through data such as

- **Wearable sensors** that track biometric data like muscle activation, sleep quality, recovery, and stress levels
- **Biometric analysis** to evaluate biomechanics, recovery biomarkers, and metabolic function

- **Genomic and epigenetic profiling** to tailor nutrition and training based on genetic predispositions
- **Real-time feedback** to personalize training down to the cellular level

Advanced AI tools analyze this detailed data to create **hyper-personalized workout plans** that help members reach peak performance. Gyms can use and analyze this data to provide hyper-personalized biohacked training plans designed specifically for the user's potential.

Nutrigenomics is a notable form of biohacking, examining how diet interacts with your unique genetic structure to optimize nutrition and meal planning.

AI-driven systems incorporate health monitoring device data to monitor various health parameters like sleep, HRV, calories, VO_2 max, and more while AI predictive models can forecast potential injuries based on biometric trends.

More advanced examples like implantable tech include magnets or microchips embedded under the skin, for more advanced health analysis.

For fitness businesses, embracing biohacking services can provide a strong competitive edge, attract a younger demographic, and position your brand within the next-generation wellness players.

Experience Economy

In today's experience-driven economy, fitness clubs redefine workouts by **offering immersive experiences** that go far beyond traditional fitness. Instead of simply providing access to equipment, gyms are creating environments that engage, motivate, and inspire members.

This shift, known as "*experience economy*," focuses on **providing value-rich experiences** rather than just selling services. In the fitness industry, this can mean, for example, cycling classes with real-time leaderboards, where participants compete with classmates or group workouts enhanced by technology. Such elements turn exercise into an interactive, game-like experience that fuels motivation and encourages repeat visits. This **personalized feedback** helps participants stay within optimal training zones, making each workout feel both tailored and rewarding.

By focusing on these enhanced experiences, fitness centers are meeting modern consumer expectations delivering not just a service but impact, emotion, and a lasting connection.

Gym Management Software

The **global gym management software market** is experiencing rapid growth, projected to reach **US$1.1 billion by 2030**, with a compound annual growth rate (CAGR) of **12.84%**. This surge is driven by rising demand for seamless, AI-powered fitness experiences and improved operational efficiency across gyms, fitness centers, and boutique studios. Between 2025 and 2029 alone, the market is expected to expand by **US$201.5 million**, according to Technavio. As shown in Figure 2-4, the GMS market is projected to expand by USD 201.5 million between 2025 and 2029, reflecting steady growth in digital fitness solutions.

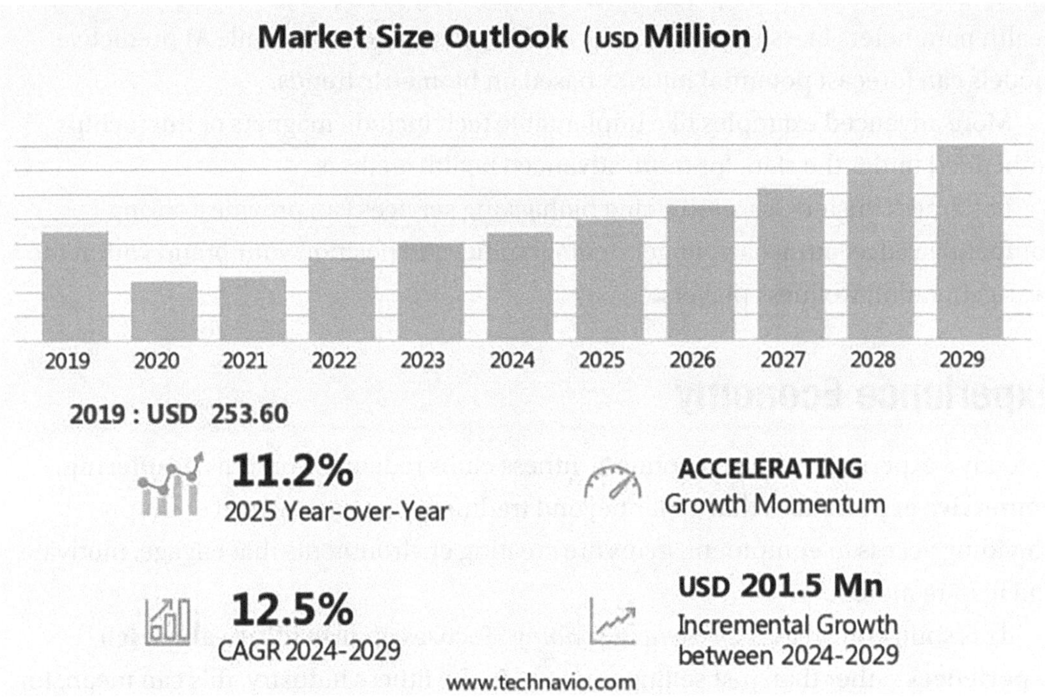

Figure 2-4. *Gym management software market 2025–2029 report by Technavio. Available at:* `https://www.technavio.com/report/gym-management-software-market-industry-analysis`

By 2026, **automation** will be a standard expectation, ranging from mobile app check-ins and contactless payments to syncing of gym workouts with mobile activity for effortless progress monitoring.

Gym management software tools help fitness studios or gyms to

- Manage member records and scheduling
- Deliver targeted communications
- Improve engagement through analytics-driven insights
- Monitor business performance via membership analytics
- Explore corporate partnerships by offering fitness apps with social and gamified features

Modern gym management systems (GMSs) like Mindbody, Trainerize, Glofox, and Zen Planner go beyond basic scheduling, including

- **CRM (Customer Relationship Management) and Scheduling Tools** – Integrated booking, billing, and client relationship management
- **Seamless Data Synchronization** – Ensuring member data is updated across all systems in real time
- **Custom White-Label Mobile Apps** – Extending digital engagement with branded experiences
- **Advanced Analytics** – Tracking member engagement, retention, and revenue trends

Automation is no longer a differentiator – it is an **expectation**. For fitness businesses, it will reduce staffing needs, lower operational costs, and create smoother, more enjoyable experiences for members. Fitness club owners should grab this competitive advantage to **retain members and outperform competitors** in the coming years.

Workout NFTs and Web3

Modern fitness businesses are beginning to leverage **Web3 technologies** to create new revenue streams and deliver innovative digital experiences.

Web3 technologies now allow creative ways to engage digital-native generations through

- **NFT (Non-Fungible Token)-Based Workouts** – Exclusive workout plans as NFTs with lifetime access, personal coaching, and other benefits.

  → *Example: Lympo creates athlete NFTs tied to premium content.*

- **Decentralized Communities** - By using **DAO** (Decentralized Autonomous Organization), members co-own fitness brands, vote on workout plans, and earn rewards with tokens.

  → *Platforms like Stepn and Genopets combine fitness with token incentives.*

- **Metaverse Gyms** - Virtual spaces in Decentraland for immersive workouts and community training.

  → *OliveX is leading with a full fitness metaverse ecosystem.*

- **Move-to-Earn Apps** - Apps reward users with crypto for physical activity, turning movement into digital value.

These technologies are especially appealing to digital-native generations who value flexibility and community-driven content. Web3 enables fitness clubs to build deeper engagement and implement creative monetization models, keeping pace with the next-generation fitness audience.

Live Streaming Classes

Social media is a powerful tool to promote your fitness business, but live streaming classes take it to the next level.

Live streaming platforms like Instagram Live, Livestream by Vimeo, Muvi, etc., allow fitness professionals to **broadcast workouts in real time** while creating opportunities for **direct interaction**.

Trainers can stream live classes, answer questions, and offer workout tips, converting followers into future clients - this showcases your expertise and expands your reach beyond your physical location.

Advanced platforms like Vimeo OTT, TrainHeroic, or TrueCoach support

- **HD live sessions** with coaching overlays
- **Real-time feedback** (pace, heart rate, reps, power output)
- **Post-workout analytics** that highlight performance and improvement areas
- **Custom workout builders** with drag-and-drop easy method

These features make virtual classes more interactive enhancing both client experience and fitness brand presence. This is a simple but effective way to generate buzz around your fitness brand and scale your reach in today's digital fitness world.

Staff and Client Apps

Staff and client management apps are getting more attention in the fitness industry. With these mobile applications, fitness clubs can streamline their offer and give fitness clients a more convenient method to work out.

For fitness clubs, the best way to benefit is to use separate apps for clients and staff to keep each aspect of your business independent and more efficient.

While desktop software handles core gym operations, a **mobile staff app** adds convenience. Your team can manage schedules, bookings, and client communication on the go - whether at the gym, at home, or off-site. The app is updated in real time when clients cancel or reschedule, while staff can message clients, confirm waivers, adjust availability, track attendance, and even accept payments, or sell products directly through the app.

Most software providers include a **basic client app**, but upgrading to a custom-branded app can significantly boost your gym's visibility. A customized app puts your logo and colors on your clients' home screens, building brand recognition and making your gym part of their daily routine. Beyond looks, it adds convenience with features like class booking, payments, waivers, rewards, and progress tracking.

It also streamlines communication, making it easy for clients to leave reviews, refer friends, and stay engaged. If you're looking to strengthen loyalty, increase revenue, and enhance client experience, a branded app is a smart investment.

We're living in a modern digital era witnessing dynamic innovation shifts in the fitness industry - staying current with technology becomes a necessity as those who adapt will thrive.

As tech continues to reshape how we train, connect, and grow, embracing these trends is the key to staying relevant, competitive, and delivering real value to today's fitness consumers.

2.4 Key Takeaways

- Fitness has evolved from basic conditioning in the 1940s–1960s to the 1970s "home workout" boom. The 1980s brought a cultural fitness revolution led by Jane Fonda's workout video tapes, while the 1990s–2010s brought diversity of fitness disciplines (e.g., CrossFit, pole dance). During the 2010s, fitness experienced its first digital integration steps, and since the 2020s, "Omnifitness" approach blends traditional training with digital technology.
- Hybrid fitness trends blend in-person training with digital tools providing more personalized experiences:
    - The number one hybrid fitness trend is **wearable technology** (heart rate, performance, etc.), which opened the door to data-driven coaching.
    - The same way, **hybrid fitness platforms and smart gyms** combine live and digital experiences through mobile apps, integrated memberships, and gamification elements.
    - **Augmented and virtual reality (AR/VR) and metaverse** redefined the way people experience fitness today. VR immerses users in gamified workout and joined virtual classes with motion capture and real-time syncing. On the other hand, AR enhances the reality of fitness experience via AR-enabled glasses or a smartphone and can be used for interactive fitness challenges.
    - **Smart fitness equipment**, from AI-powered machines to interactive cardio gear, offers real-time workout analysis, which also expanded into smart workout apparel and portable gear that integrate biometric and muscle activity sensors.
    - **Gamified fitness** is another rising trend that boosts user engagement by turning workouts into interactive experiences
    - All these trends resulted in a **holistic health** approach – integration of overall wellness into workout culture, being the most important one in today's fitness hybrid landscape.

- Software fitness trends:
    - **AI-powered apps and AI-driven programs** can create new engagement models, from virtual training memberships to hybrid coaching services.
    - **Biohacking** combines data-driven decision-making and modern tech to optimize overall well-being through data such as wearable devices, biometric analysis, and genomic profiling. This data helps professionals create hyper-personalized workout regimens that help members reach peak performance.
    - The shift, known as "***experience economy***," focuses on providing value-rich experiences rather than just selling services. In the fitness industry, this personalized feedback helps participants stay within optimal training zones.
    - **Gym management software** tools help fitness studios or gyms deliver personalized training while running a business including CRM and scheduling tools, seamless data synchronization, custom mobile apps, and advanced analytics.
    - **Web3 technologies** now allow creative ways to engage digital-native generations through NFT based workouts, decentralized communities by using DAO, metaverse gyms, and move-to-earn apps.
    - **Live streaming classes** take it to the next level. Live streaming platforms allow fitness professionals to broadcast workouts in real time while creating opportunities for direct interaction.
    - A **mobile staff app** helps gym professionals and staff to handle core gym operations while a basic **client mobile app** adds convenience with features like class booking, payments, waivers, rewards, and progress tracking. If you're looking to strengthen loyalty, increase revenue, and enhance client experience, a branded app is a smart investment.

CHAPTER 3

How to Stay Ahead of the Curve

Chapter 3 casts light on how you can keep pace with the dynamic fitness technology, no matter if you work in the fitness industry or just interested in keeping an active lifestyle.

Staying up to date with technology trends is no longer optional for fitness businesses and clients – it is crucial for growth and long-term success. As fitness habits and needs evolve, gym owners and trainers must adapt to stay relevant. Whether it's integrating new tools, offering unique experiences, or optimizing operations, staying abreast can be the difference between a thriving studio and the one that falls behind.

3.1 Why Is Staying Up to Date Highly Important in the Fitness Sector?

From wearables and mobile apps to home training, fitness technology changes the way people train and how gyms operate. Early adopters in the fitness industry will gain a significant advantage, offering more convenient and personalized services. For example, digital check-ins, class booking apps, etc., facilitate training for both clients and staff – clients can book or cancel their class without any hassle, and it helps trainers focus on coaching instead of admin work.

Gym management tools can streamline billing, scheduling, and member engagement. Features like automated notifications, online booking, or payment can help reduce operational costs without compromising service. Technology also allows better supplier negotiations, resource allocation, and overhead management, all of which support healthier profit margins. Apps that connect to memberships or track workouts keep users motivated, while **virtual classes and loyalty programs** can enhance

M. Dakić, *When Fitness Goes Tech*, https://doi.org/10.1007/979-8-8688-2457-9_3

retention. Collecting feedback, offering personalized offers, and building community through social media helps you meet your audience where they are and keep them coming back. Creating a standout customer experience is also easier with tech – **loyalty programs, personalized offers, and app-based communication** build deeper connections and foster retention.

A successful gym also depends on the quality of its staff and the safety of its environment. Staying updated with **best practices in recruitment, onboarding, and training** ensures your team is aligned with your values and goals. Creating job descriptions, fostering team building, and **educating staff** on new tools and procedures make for a stronger, more unified team. Safety-wise, investing in access control, proper lighting, equipment training, and emergency protocols protects both your clients and your brand. Software that tracks customer engagement allows owners to reward loyalty, identify gaps, and customize offers to increase visits. With the right data, you can tailor experiences, optimize class schedules, and provide services that meet your members' needs, driving both satisfaction and growth.

In today's digital world, a strong online presence is no longer optional. Effective marketing strategies require an understanding of your audience, current trends, and clear campaign goals. From social media promotions and referral incentives to content creation like workout videos and testimonials, modern marketing tools help studios build brand awareness and stand out.

To stay ahead of the curve, you will need a combination of tech awareness and strategic actions. Start with staying informed on the tools that reshape the fitness industry like

- **AI and Machine Learning (ML)**: Personalized training, diet plans, and chatbots
- **Wearables and IoT**: Smartwatches, fitness trackers, connected equipment
- **AR/VR**: Immersive workouts, gamification
- **Mobile Apps and On-Demand Platforms**: Custom content, live classes
- **Blockchain and NFTs**: Loyalty programs, digital ownership, and gamification

Both fitness professionals and clients can follow such trends via Product Hunt, TechCrunch, FitTech Insider, or specialized newsletters to stay informed on new trends and innovations in the industry.

Collect and analyze customer data to offer personalized training and track engagement and retention.

Experiment with automation tools to save time and scale, for example, *ChatGPT* for customer support or training plans, *Zapier/Axiom* for admin automation, and various AI video tools (e.g., *Pictory, Synthesia*) for content creation.

Whether you run a gym, offer online classes, or sell fitness products, develop a digital strategy. You can develop a mobile app and offer hybrid memberships (*digital + in-person*) and use online communities (*Discord, Instagram groups, etc.*) to boost engagement.

Another way is to partner with tech startups to gain early access to innovation, test new tools, and co-create digital products or even challenges.

To keep pace with the dynamic shift of trends in the fitness industry, the job is not done unless you regularly collect feedback, make changes based on data, and test your ideas with small pilot groups prior to going public. This data can fuel targeted promotions, loyalty programs, and personalized offers that boost retention and increase visit frequency.

All the abovementioned methods to stay ahead are worth nothing unless you invest to upskill your fitness staff. You can help your employees and coaches by taking online courses (*Coursera, FitTech Academy, etc.*), attending fitness tech expos, and joining industry groups like FitTech Club and Wearable Tech World.

Besides offering innovative services and offers, do not forget about the foundation – safety and security. Ensure your facilities are clean and well lit with clearly marked exits. Provide your members with all the equipment, add-ons, and perks before going digital. Basic fitness needs need to be met; thus, build your fitness business steadily managing foundation first and then moving on to other upgrades.

In conclusion, leveraging technology empowers fitness businesses to stay competitive and connected in a constantly evolving market. Create a member-focused business by combining strong branding, strategy planning, and smart technology, and your business will thrive in a dynamic/competitive market.

3.2 How to Adapt to Changing Fitness Technology

Keeping pace with advancements in fitness technology is essential to delivering better and more engaging experiences for members.

If You Are a Fitness Professional

Before you start planning digital, define the current state of your business. By analyzing various aspects of your business, such as performance, processes, resources, etc., you can identify your strengths and weaknesses. This will help you determine which areas of your business need improvement. Digital tools today allow fitness clubs to automate business processes, work remotely with clients, and generate consistent income all year round.

Determine Your Needs

Before integrating new technologies, **assess your existing condition**:

- *What software do you use, if any?*
- *Do you leverage tools like CRM, wearables, automated payment, etc.?*
- *Are there any tools connected to streamline operations?*
- *Do you have a website or a mobile app?*

Evaluate what is outdated or underused like booking systems, CRMs, or marketing tools. **Explore fitness digital tools** so you can invest in scalable software (e.g., *scheduling, member tracking, mobile apps*) that will meet your business needs. You can create a poll for your members and gather feedback on what they would appreciate the most (e.g., *wearables, remote classes, or online booking*) and start with gradual steps to make the entire process sustainable.

It may seem demanding at first, but this important step lays the foundation for a future change. Once you get a clear picture on your **business digital maturity**, you will be prepared to begin implementing improvements.

Stay Informed

Subscribe to fitness tech newsletter and join similar communities or forums (LinkedIn, Reddit) to watch for emerging trends that would suit your own needs. **Keep up with fitness trends** through seminars, expert content, or digital communities as it will help identify new methods to upgrade your services. If possible, attend expo events like IHRSA or FIBO, for more insight into what's gaining popularity in digital fitness innovations.

Check how other fitness clubs innovate and how their digital offer works for the audience.

Embrace Hybrid Fitness Models

Offer online classes via platforms like Zoom, Vimeo, or TrainHeroic for live or recorded sessions, and provide remote options for members who travel frequently or prefer to train at home. A hybrid business model can include livestreamed classes, on-demand content, or remote coaching keeping the members active no matter their location or schedule.

A great idea is to develop your **branded mobile app** for bookings, progress tracking, rewards, and more.

Finally, understanding your audience is the key to success - monitoring **client preferences and goals** will enable you to adjust services.

Personalize Member Experience

The most effective way to **enhance your members' experience is through data**. The data gathered via fitness trackers and wearables allow trainers to monitor real-time progress and create customized workout plans that adapt as the user improves. Leverage such data (*attendance, preferences*) to **offer tailored workouts** and nutrition tips and boost engagement.

Use technology to **collect and analyze feedback** through surveys and app ratings. By tracking campaign performance, website visits, and social engagement, you can identify what works great and which parts need to be improved. These insights will help refine your marketing and keep your business aligned with member expectations.

Strong customer engagement is a key differentiator in a competitive market. Use gathered data to keep your members' motivation high - introduce leaderboards, community challenges, or rewards, and it will turn workout routines into interactive experiences. Such **personalized incentives and reward-based systems** can boost client retention and create a sense of community.

Educate Your Team and Members

Ensure that your trainers and reception staff are confident to use new tools and features - educate them on how **to incorporate wearables/AI** tools into their programs and how to **onboard members** for digital tools.

Foster a culture that is open to communication and ongoing learning as it will be the key to staying ahead of the curve.

Prepare Your Business for the Future

If you wish to prepare for the future, **implement wearable technology** for more insights and explore other trends that can help your fitness club.

Apple Watch, Fitbit, or WHOOP integration will bring you better performance insights while long-term investments like NFT-based memberships or virtual club spaces can enhance your position beyond the local market.

Automate where possible from marketing emails to smart lighting - whenever you automate repetitive tasks, you will save your time and costs in the long run.

Staying up to date isn't just about using trendy tech; it's about evolving with the industry and meeting your members' expectations. No matter if through digital integration or new training formats, staying up to date with market shifts will ensure your business remains relevant in the market.

The key to staying ahead of the curve lies in ongoing education and smart investments - invest in modern equipment and software as it will improve your customer satisfaction and retention.

If You Are a Fitness Client and Enthusiast

Adapting to changing fitness technology as a **fitness client or user** means being curious about the tools that can improve your fitness journey.

Here are a few suggested tips to stay ahead.

Define Your Goals

Ask yourself what your fitness goal is – to lose weight, get stronger, sleep better, or manage stress, or all of these. Once you define your goals, it will be easier to choose a **fitness tech to match your needs**.

For example:

Goal	Tech Tool Example
Home workouts	*Peloton, Apple Fitness+*
Habit Tracking	*MyFitnessPal, Strava, Strong*
Stress and mindfulness	*Fitbit Sense, Calm*
Sleep and recovery	*WHOOP, Oura Ring*

Stay in the Loop

If you wish to gain faster results, follow **fitness tech blogs** (e.g., *Wearable, TechCrunch, Wired, Trainerize*), your fitness studio newsletter, or local blogs, if any. You can also **join fitness communities** like on Reddit (e.g., *r/fitness and similar*) or Facebook groups dedicated to fitness wearables and apps.

Try Before You Buy

Before you choose any fitness tech or application, you can try and **test it** through

- Free trials (e.g., *Apple Fitness+, Fitbit*)
- Demo sessions with new gear at your local gym (e.g., *VR, wearables*) or
- Renting fitness devices, as some stores offer short-term wearable rentals

Consult Your Trainer

Once you get your workout data, treat it **as guidance** to adjust your training. Metrics like *step count, HRV, and recovery scores* are helpful, but they vary daily so the best option would be to ask your trainer how to interpret your data and improve workouts.

If your trainers are familiar with your tech (e.g., *Garmin or WHOOP*), they will help you to align the tech tips with your training plan. Many professionals offer tech-integrated coaching and help interpret your metrics better than an app.

Adapt When Needed

Keep in mind that your fitness goals will change with time, so **reassess** every few months if the tool **is still helpful** in achieving your fitness goals. Be flexible and switch tech tools once your goals shift (e.g., *from weight loss to conditioning*).

No matter how helpful, the tech tools can cause fatigue so make sure you **practice digital balance**. Unplug regularly and use tools that support mindful movement (apps that have rest days and personalized pacing, not compulsory tracking).

From smart wearables to interactive apps, staying updated with fitness digital trends can bring great advantages to both fitness professionals and clients.

See Table 3-1 for tips on leveraging digital tools, whether as a fitness user or a professional.

Table 3-1. *How to keep up with the digital fitness trends – tips for fitness professionals and users. Source: Created by the author*

HOW TO KEEP UP WITH FITNESS TRENDS

IF YOU ARE A FITNESS PROFESSIONAL	IF YOU ARE A FITNESS USER
DETERMINE YOUR BUSINESS NEEDS	DEFINE YOUR FITNESS GOALS
KEEP UP WITH FITNESS TRENDS	STAY IN THE LOOP
EMBRACE HYBRID FITNESS MODELS	'TRY BEFORE YOU BUY'
PERSONALIZE MEMBER EXPERIENCE	CONSULT YOUR TRAINER
EDUCATE YOUR TEAM AND MEMBERS	ADAPT WHEN NECESSARY
PREPARE YOUR BUSINESS FOR FUTURE	PRACTICE DIGITAL BALANCE

The fitness industry has opened new opportunities for people to stay active and healthy. From smart wearables to interactive apps, staying updated with fitness digital trends can bring great advantages to both fitness professionals and clients.

Digital solutions remove common barriers – **for fitness providers**, this opens new ways to reach clients beyond the gym floor. As innovation accelerates, so do client expectations; hence, offering advanced tools like virtual coaching, AI-driven programs, or hybrid membership models demonstrates your commitment to quality.

Ultimately, the fusion of technology and fitness will enable **fitness users** to take greater control over their health, develop sustainable habits, and lead more balanced lives.

3.3 Key Takeaways

- From wearables and mobile apps to home training, fitness technology has changed the way people train and gyms operate. Early adopters in the fitness industry will gain a significant advantage, offering more convenient and personalized services. Staying updated with best practices in recruitment, onboarding, and training will ensure your team is aligned with your values. To stay ahead of the curve, both fitness professionals and enthusiasts will need a combination of tech awareness and strategic actions.
- From smart wearables to interactive apps, staying updated with fitness digital trends can bring great advantages to both fitness professionals and clients.
    - If you are a fitness professional
        - Determine your needs and evaluate existing business condition
        - Stay informed
        - Embrace hybrid fitness models
        - Personalize member experience
        - Educate your team and staff
        - Prepare your business for the future
    - If you are a fitness enthusiast
        - Stay in the loop
        - Define your goals
        - Try before you buy
        - Consult your trainer
        - Adapt when needed
- For **fitness providers**, digital solutions remove common barriers and open up new ways to reach clients beyond the gym floor. The fusion of technology and fitness will enable **fitness users** to take greater control over their health, develop sustainable habits, and lead more balanced lives.

CHAPTER 4

For Fitness Entrepreneurs

Chapter 4 is intended for fitness entrepreneurs and professionals working in the fitness industry, sports management, or personal coaching.

You will learn about the benefits of the gym management system (GMS) and how to choose the best one for your business needs. You will gain insights on how business mobile applications (*staff vs. client apps*) can help your business grow and improve user experience. Finally, if you are a personal trainer, you will learn how to provide tailored fitness programming through smart devices, ensuring user satisfaction.

Before jumping directly into the world of gym management software (GMS), it is important to first understand the current trends and opportunities in the fitness industry. The market is filled with innovative possibilities for aspiring fitness entrepreneurs, no matter if you run boutique fitness studios or large fitness facilities.

To begin digital adoption, conduct a detailed fitness market research and identify gaps in your business – e.g., *are there any popular fitness trends to implement, is there a specific audience that current offerings fail to serve,* and similar (see the section "How to Adapt to Changing Fitness Technology" in Chapter 3). Once you understand the current trends and determine gaps in your business, you will be able to position your fitness club for success.

The evolving fitness industry offers a plethora of options which can help you streamline operations and improve client engagement, no matter the type of fitness business you run.

Before we go further, let's first list diverse business models of a modern fitness digital ecosystem:

- **Traditional Gyms** – *Medium- to large-scale facilities, broad equipment, and optional class packages*
- **Boutique Fitness Studios** – *Specialized, focusing on one or two types of fitness disciplines, e.g., barre, pole dance, calisthenics*
- **Yoga Studios** – *Dedicated to various forms of yoga classes*

M. Dakić, *When Fitness Goes Tech*, https://doi.org/10.1007/979-8-8688-2457-9_4

- **Pilates Studios** - *Specialized places for Pilates classes*
- **Martial Art Dojos** - *For example, karate, jiu-jitsu, etc., from small-, medium- to large-scale facilities*
- **CrossFit Boxes** - *HIIT workout gyms, powerlifting*
- **Dance Studios** - *Ballet, classic, and modern dance*
- **Aerobics Centers** - *Aerobics classes, with or no fitness gear*
- **Personal Training Studios** - *Small-scale*
- **Boot Camps** - *Outdoor/indoor group programs, boot camp style*
- **Sports Training Facilities** - *Specific sports like tennis, basketball, etc.*
- **Climbing Gyms** - *Indoor facilities for rock climbing*
- **Boxing and Kickboxing Gyms** - *Boxing and kickboxing trainings*
- **Swimming Schools** - *Swimming schools + aquatic workouts like water aerobics, etc.*
- **Health and Wellness Retreats** - *Holistic health, fitness classes + nutrition guidance + relaxation techniques*
- **Virtual Fitness Platforms** - *Live or pre-recorded workout classes*
- **Fitness Apps** - *Mobile/web apps for tracking, workouts, and nutrition*
- **Athletic Recovery Centers** - *Recovery like cryotherapy or massage and physical therapy, chiropractic services*
- **Senior Fitness Centers** - *For the older population and safe workouts*
- **Kids' Fitness Centers** - *Correct posture and proper physical development*
- **Corporate Wellness Programs** - *Fitness + wellness for corporate entities*
- **Fitness Equipment Sales/Rentals** - *Selling or renting out fitness equipment*
- **Fitness Supplement Stores** - *Fitness supplements, condiments, and accessories*

There are probably more business models with their own specific needs, and this **diversity is the reason why the market offers a wide range of digital fitness solutions** – harnessing the power of digital tools will help you run your business more efficiently.

When talking about types of fitness software, most of the solutions offer similar functionalities, features, or capabilities. The key differences lie in the **size of the business, the deployment method, and the operating system (OS) supported** by each platform.

There are some fitness software solutions that support several operating systems and businesses of all sizes. Examples include WellnessLiving, designed for wellness studios of all sizes, and Pike13, supporting all three major operating systems.

However, there are also systems designed to serve small to medium-sized businesses (SMBs) where some support multiple operating systems while others support one or two major operating systems, like MINDBODY and EZFacility.

You can also find fitness digital solutions that serve only small businesses but still support more than one operating system, like Fitune, Everfit, etc., and those only available as on-premises solutions like Club Sentry which supports only Microsoft Windows but can serve businesses of all sizes.

The outline of fitness digital solutions and business models shows the increasing technology adoption in the modern fitness industry. From boutique studios to large fitness enterprises, technology is no longer optional if you wish for your business to remain viable.

Today, the fitness sector represents a field where technology plays a primary role in securing long-term success and competitive market advantage. As shown in Figure 4-1, modern workout planning often integrates digital performance tracking with physical training environments.

Figure 4-1. *Man preparing for a workout. Image by rawpixel.com from Freepik. Source:* `https://www.freepik.com/`

4.1 Gym Management System (GMS) – What Is It and How Does It Work

Gym management system (GMS) has become a priority in the fitness industry as it enables you to run your gym more efficiently, from automation of administrative tasks and class scheduling to staff management and payment processing.

Gym management system (GMS) is a digital solution designed to streamline the daily operations of a gym or a fitness center. It blends different systems into a single platform, customized for fitness businesses. Most GMSs are cloud based, meaning they do not require local installation as you can access it online via a web browser or a dedicated app.

Gym staff and owners have a separate **administrative dashboard** to manage their specific day-to-day operations while gym members have a **client app** to view class schedules, book classes, make payments, or manage their membership details.

The GMS acts like a centralized database for member information (*contact details, payment history, attendance records, etc.*), enabling you to tailor offerings to individual member needs. It helps you run a business, covering several key aspects like *membership management, booking and scheduling classes, sales prospecting, customer satisfaction/ retention,* and *advanced analytics.*

For effective **membership management**, GMS enables paperless signups, simplifying the entire process. As professionals, you have a user-friendly dashboard with all relevant member information along with tools for communication and payment in just a few clicks. GMS also enables your staff to book members or cancel prior bookings via any device, thus reducing scheduling errors.

GMS helps you create **marketing campaigns** and collect potential clients to reach out to with promotional membership offers. These features are also beneficial for your club members - you can send personalized messages tailored to specific categories like class attendance or membership types.

GMS also works as a reporting tool with **advanced analytics** - you can easily generate various reports, e.g., *on current members, debtors, or failed billing.* Such key performance indicator (KPI) reports will provide valuable insights to help you assess your gym's performance and define your future goals.

In technical terms, GMS is usually offered as a cloud-based SaaS (*Software as a Service*), but it can also be self-hosted on your own servers for more control, but with higher maintenance costs. Frontend typically includes a *web admin app + mobile/web app for members and staff.* Backend manages *core business logic (billing, notifications,* etc.) while depending on external services for payments (*Stripe, PayPal, Apple Pay, etc.*), messaging (*Twilio, FireBase Cloud Messaging, etc.*), analytics (*Google Analytics, Mixpanel, etc.*), and similar.

Gym Management System – User Journeys

For fitness members, the process is simple and intuitive.

Registration

The process begins when a new user joins the gym, completing a **digital registration** form. Upon submission, the system automatically generates a **digital waiver**, creates a **member profile**, and securely stores payment credentials. When a member profile is created, the system sends out an automated welcome message confirming the enrolment.

Booking

Members need to **access a mobile application** to view available classes and book the one they want to attend. Once they book, the system updates class capacity and sends a confirmation notification (*SMS, email, etc.*). In case the class is full, you can set a feature for users to join a waitlist.

Check-In

When members come for a class, they complete **check-in** by scanning a QR code or via staff confirmation. These attendance records are stored in the system which you can later use for loyalty programs or similar gym incentives.

Payment Management

The system tracks **all payments** and in case of any missed payments, the billing system attempts an automatic retry. If failed, the system sends a notification to the member and can restrict member access or mark the account.

Event Transactions

Members can buy tickets for special events through an integrated **point-of-sale (POS)** system or **online stores**. Upon transaction, a digital ticket or QR code is sent to a member (*email/SMS*), and the list is updated in real time, providing accurate event planning.

Check Figure 4-2 to get a clear diagram of user journeys (*members/trainers*) in a gym management software.

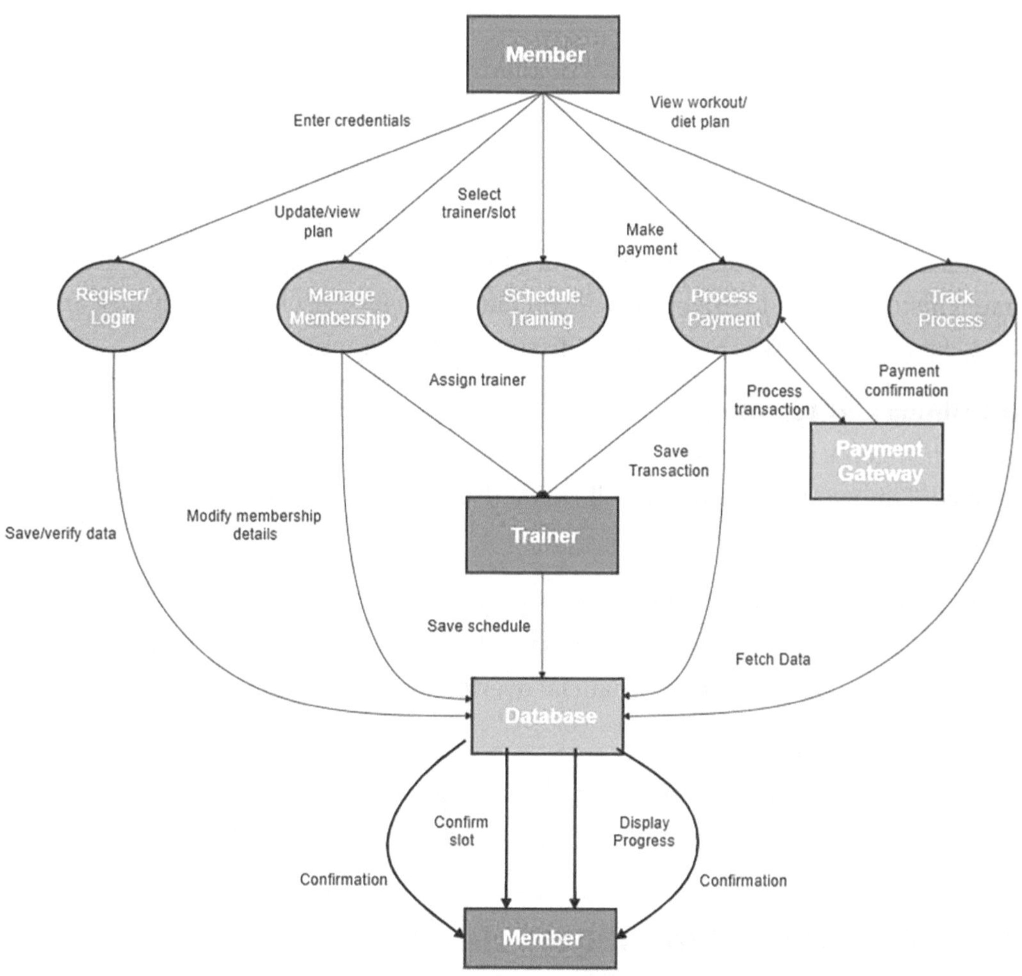

Figure 4-2. *Gym management software flowchart (Khan, Q.) by EdrawMax. Available at:* *`https://www.edrawmax.com/templates/data-flow-diagram-for-gym-management-system-1064290/`*

For fitness entrepreneurs, always start simple.

Initial Implementation

Start with a simple configuration and prioritize features for **your** business needs (*online booking, automated billing, performance tracking, etc.*). You can add more advanced modules (*CRM or retail integrations*) once the core processes are stable.

Validation of Billing Workflows

Focus on payment processing, as errors in billing directly affect financial performance and damage member trust. A critical early step is to test billing flows as mistakes in this section cost money and trust.

Data Migration

When transitioning from existing tools, you should carefully map member records and payment histories prior to import. Once you map the fields, migrate cleanly and export existing data securely. This reduces any discrepancies in member data.

Staff Training and Adoption

Even when systems are user-friendly, staff training and consistent operating procedures are crucial. Train your staff since a well-defined structure for system use minimizes errors and improves liability.

System Scope and Feature Selection

Do not overload your system with unnecessary features or pay for tools you will never actually use. This will prevent any financial overload and operational disruptions.

Policy Configuration

Integrate transparent *cancellation* and *no-show* policies within the system and clearly communicate these rules to members to reduce administrative burden.

Limitations of Gym Management Software

Adoption of GMS does not come without challenges - certain technical, operational, or user-related issues can occur and affect the efficiency of these systems.

1. **Technical Issues**

   Cloud-based platforms depend on stable Internet connection and in case of server **outages**, your staff may not be able to, for example, access the system. Integration with third-party services (*payment/analytics*) may fail, causing billing errors, misreporting, or **discrepancies across systems**. Also **poorly designed** user interfaces can lead to booking errors or increased member churn.

2. **Expense Considerations**

    The cost of GMS can be a serious challenge, especially for smaller gyms with limited budgets. Subscription fees can increase with the **add-ons** or **premium features** (*members/additional features*), setup, onboarding**,** and training fees. **Hardware components** (e.g., *tablets, upgraded network infrastructure*) also contribute to total costs.

3. **Learning Curve**

    When you adopt new software, you must onboard your staff - it may impact operational efficiency as training sessions **consume** their **time** and may **require external resources**. **Staff turnover** can further trigger repeated training cycles.

4. **Data Security Issues**

    GMS stores sensitive information and any **security gaps** or **poor access controls** can expose data to unauthorized access. Mitigation requires encryption, multi-factor authentication, role-based access, regular updates, and third-party security audits.

5. **Data Management Issues**

    Integration with other software can cause **synchronization problems** between, for example, *booking apps and POS systems*, resulting in reporting inaccuracies. To avoid this, select platforms with standardized APIs, real-time synchronization, centralized data repositories, and regular validation procedures.

6. **Low Customizability**

    Certain GMS platforms offer **limited customization** options where standard features may not fit your membership or class structures. Such limitations can affect both operational efficiency and member experience. Select systems with modular features and robust API support to alleviate these constraints.

7. **Insufficient Customer Service**

   Inadequate customer service (*delayed response times, limited availability, etc.*) can cause payment errors or system misconfigurations, while poor **support** can potentially lead to inconsistent staff practices. Evaluating providers for responsiveness, expertise, and availability is essential to mitigate this risk.

8. **User Experience Challenges**

   Complicated interfaces, **non-intuitive workflows**, or device incompatibility can slow your staff performing daily tasks, reducing both staff and member satisfaction. Choose platforms with intuitive design, cross-device compatibility, and opportunities for usability testing to help ensure smooth operation.

While gym management system (GMS) offers numerous operational advantages, these challenges highlight why you need to choose your vendor carefully, onboard your staff properly, and implement clear mitigation strategies.

Understanding these limitations will prepare you for an effective implementation of a GMS to support your long-term business success.

4.2 Key Features of a Gym Management System and How to Choose One for Your Needs?

Prior to choosing any gym management software (GMS), the best is to do your own research on the key features of the platform you would like to use, as some platforms may have the features that support your business needs, while others may not.

Still, there is a set of features that is common for this kind of software solutions, so let's check some standard features for most GMSs.

Staff and Member App

A mobile application is the key feature of modern GMS, improving operational efficiency for both members and staff.

Members can book classes, receive updates, and manage their memberships easily. You can integrate access control within the app, allowing members to enter the facility using a generated QR code.

Staff app consolidates all operational tasks in a single platform for your staff. They can monitor equipment or their class schedules, record attendance, etc., directly via mobile. This improves internal communication via automated messaging and notifications.

Together, member and staff mobile apps create a consolidated system that streamlines business operations and improves member experience.

Membership Management

Most GMSs are cloud solutions and hence must maintain compliance with regulations like General Data Protection Regulation (GDPR) due to sensitive data storing.

You can automate processes like **recurring billing** and **renewal notifications which** reduces administrative workload. According to a study by McKinsey, automation in financial aspects can increase productivity by up to **40%**, reducing missed payments and improving cash flow.

With digital onboarding tools, you help members securely **sign agreements and liability waivers electronically**, where each document is encrypted and stored within the system. This simplifies the onboarding process, allowing your staff to focus more on service quality and member engagement.

Attendance and Access Control

GMS enables you to monitor attendance in real time through integrated check-in systems (*QR codes, RFID [radio-frequency identification] cards, etc.*) and obtain data on training attendance and engagement levels. Such data provide a clear overview of member behavior - you can identify the most popular classes or detect members who may lose motivation and act, for example, by offering personalized promotions. As shown in Figure 4-3, modern gym management software dashboards provide an integrated overview of member activity, scheduling, and operational metrics.

Figure 4-3. *Dashboard of a gym management system. Created by Joy UI.UX. Available at:* `https://dribbble.com/shots/25023184-Redbelt-Gym-Management-CRM`

Scheduling and Class Management

Your administrators can easily create, organize, and publish class schedules for both members and trainers, visible on all linked platforms in real time.

You can assign trainers to specific sessions based on their expertise, availability, and workload or send automated notifications on any cancellations, reducing last-minute disruptions. If any of your classes shows as particularly popular, you can add the waitlist feature to handle the capacity automatically.

The entire process is simplified for **members,** and the automation not only provides better user experience but also helps you optimize class management.

Billing and Payment Processing

With **automated invoicing**, the system generates and sends invoices according to each member's plan (*class package or one-time purchase*). With integrated payment gateways, you enable members to **make payments securely** via credit or debit cards, PayPal, etc. These gateways are commonly compliant with PCI DSS (*Payment Card Industry Data Security Standard*) providing the highest level of protection.

Automating these financial processes will reduce administrative workload and save operational costs.

CRM (Customer Relationship Management)

Modern GMSs offer a **CRM module**, the system that consolidates all activities and enables a personalized approach to your members.

Communication tools help you automate reminders, send promotional offers, and deliver notifications (*email, SMS, push alerts*) for regular member engagement. **Lead management** allows you to track all incoming or prospective clients, automatically schedule follow-ups, and convert them into active members.

The CRM system can also **collect feedback** though surveys, ratings, or comment forms, which you can later use to improve your future service offerings.

Reporting and Analytics

Reporting and analytics tools generate detailed **financial reports** for better financial planning and decision-making. With **attendance analytics**, you can monitor class popularity, participation, or member retention rates and identify engagement patterns and potential risks.

Performance dashboards with visually presented key performance indicators (KPIs) in real time (*e.g., revenue per member or membership growth*) provide you with actionable insights to improve your operational efficiency, as shown in Figure 4-4.

Figure 4-4. Example of a gym management system (GMS) dashboard. Source: Vagaro. Available at: `https://www.vagaro.com/en-gb/pro/gym-software`

Staff and Payroll Management

Key parts of any GMS are efficient staff and payroll management. Most systems manage detailed **trainer profiles** and store key data like certifications, class schedules, and performance analytics. Such consolidated information helps you to monitor productivity, evaluate performance, and ensure compliance with safety standards.

Automated payroll management calculates compensation precisely based on the parameters you define (*hourly rates, class attendance, or other models*). This minimizes errors and ensures timely payout for all staff members.

Shift scheduling features help you assign classes, track availability, and manage substitutions with ease. You will free up your time as a gym owner to focus on strategic growth.

Marketing and Engagement Tools

Marketing tools **automate communication** (email/SMS), allowing you to promote new classes, share announcements, or deliver personalized messages. **Loyalty and referral programs** will help you further improve member satisfaction by rewarding consistent attendance, milestone achievements, or successful referrals of new clients. Such programs not only motivate members but can also expand your studio's community through word-of-mouth promotion.

Integration with social media platforms and websites enables you to manage your online brand presence, schedule posts, and promote events directly from the GMS platform. This will help you ensure constant branding across all digital channels.

Inventory and Point of Sale (POS)

An integrated **point-of-sale (POS)** system facilitates the process of all on-site transactions (e.g., *equipment, supplements, memberships, event tickets*), so all sales are recorded accurately in real time. With **inventory tracking** tools, you can monitor stock levels of products (e.g., *apparel, accessories, nutritional products*) and prevent shortages if quantities are low.

Automation in **generating receipts** will ensure each transaction creates a digital or printed receipt, no matter if in person or online. Such automation streamlines recordkeeping for both members and staff.

With these tools, you will simplify business processes across the entire gym or studio, while keeping business operations structured and efficient.

How to Choose the Best Gym Management System

No matter what type of fitness, health, or wellness business you run or how many members you serve, having a reliable fitness software will help you manage daily operational workflows.

All fitness facilities (*small, medium, or large, public or private*) share a common goal: to offer the best quality service to their members. The most effective method is to capitalize on software solutions providing good member experience and efficient day-to-day operations.

A good fitness software provides a wide range of features, from simplifying operational processes for trainers and members to automating marketing campaigns.

To find the right software for your business, you will first need to consider a few standard functionalities like membership management, billing and scheduling management, and marketing tools.

Other features like member forums, reporting, and analytics also add value to the fitness software solution, so make sure that the platform you choose supports specific needs for your fitness business.

When choosing the best GMS for your business, here are some recommended steps to follow:

1. **Brainstorm Your Business Needs** - Write down key areas you want to improve and features your business would benefit from the most. Every business is different in size, number of members, etc., so make sure you determine exactly the features you need.

2. **Review Features** - Many fitness solutions may start with similar features, yet service requirements may vary, depending on the size and type of your business. Before selecting a solution, make sure the chosen solution offers the features you need.

3. **Compare Prices** - Look for the software that fits your budget. Check monthly and annual subscription, as you can get a better deal if you opt for an annual method. Your business needs may also change so choose a scalable solution.

4. **Read Service Terms** - Check all the terms before choosing any solution (e.g., *security, encryption and protection of client information, customer support*) and confirm relevant details related to

   a. ***Stored data***

      i. Data export (*easy data export in case you leave the app*)

      ii. Storage location (*server location - EU, United States, etc. - and if GDPR compliant*)

      iii. Third-party sharing (*if they share/sell data to partners, advertisers, etc.*)

      iv. Data ownership (*who owns client data - you or the provider*)

b. ***Payments***

i. Billing model (*subscription, per member*)

ii. Hidden fees (*any extra setup, onboarding, or integration costs*)

iii. Auto-renewal (*do they automatically renew without notice*)

iv. Refund policy (*is there a refund or cancellation fee in certain cases*)

c. ***Support***

i. Feature limitations (*if needed tools are available only in higher-pricing tiers*)

ii. Customization limitations (*can you adapt it to your needs*)

iii. Integration support (*if it integrates with payment providers, booking, or accounting tools*)

iv. Tech support (*included or additional fee, response times*)

d. ***Compliance***

i. Liability (*responsibility if a failure affected your business*)

ii. Uptime warranty (*do they commit to a minimum uptime, e.g., 99.9%*)

iii. Termination terms (*what happens to data if you cease cooperation*)

iv. Compliance (*if certified for security [ISO/SOC2] or privacy standards [GDPR]*)

5. **Request a Free Trial or Demo** – Request a demo to get a chance to assess the software and check if it integrates smoothly with your existing systems, how your members respond to it, and if it meets your business needs.

6. **Sign Up for the Service** – Once you choose the software, complete a registration, but if you opted for a custom quote, check for any available deals or special discounts that could reduce your monthly or annual payments.

Security of GMS

Securing member and staff data is the cornerstone of building trust in a fitness digital platform. GMSs, SaaS based or self-hosted, should include strong security protocols; however, you can also improve security measures as an owner through proper vendor selection and configuration.

Most reputable GMSs, such as *Fitune, Glofox,* or *Mindbody,* come with pre-integrated security layers, including

- **Data Encryption (SSL/TLS)** - Ensures all data (e.g., *payments, personal details*) is encrypted during data transfer between the app and the server
- **Secure Cloud Hosting** - Where data is stored on certified servers like AWS, Google Cloud, Azure, etc., that comply with global security standards like ISO/IEC 27001
- **Role-Based Access Control (RBAC)** - Defines who can access or edit certain data (e.g., *trainer can see attendance but not billing records*)
- **Regular Security Updates** - Regularly patch vulnerabilities and apply compliance updates automatically
- **PCI DSS Compliance** - Ensures that all payment transactions meet financial data protection standards
- **GDPR Compliance** - Ensures lawful processing of personal data for EU/EEA members, including rights to data access, modification, and deletion

However, even with strong vendor protection, I strongly advise you to take additional steps like

- **Strong Authentication Practices** - Users provide strong passwords and two-factor authentication (2FA) to get access to an app (e.g., *code, face scan, or fingerprint*).
- **Regular QA and Security Checks** - Audit your software on a regular basis to identify any vulnerabilities on time and address them.
- **Access Management** - If any of the trainers leaves or changes roles, update the system and app access instantly.

- **Device Security** - Ask for a PIN or biometric protection on staff devices that access gym systems.
- **Staff Training** - Educate instructors on handling sensitive data (e.g., *do not share member info via unsecured channels*).
- **Data Backup Policy** - Ensure data is regularly backed up securely and tested for restoration.
- **Vendor Due Diligence** - Select vendors that openly outline their security and compliance standards in documentation.
- **AI-powered tools** - These can help you analyze and define suspicious behavior.

Although most cloud-based systems handle security at their infrastructure level, **data protection is a shared responsibility** - the vendor protects the platform, but you ensure proper usage and access control. For example, a secure app cannot protect member data if your employees download private data to unprotected personal devices.

Custom vs. Ready-Made GMS

The key difference between custom and ready-made products is that with custom, you can build a platform for your specific business needs, while ready-made products come with customization limits, depending on the package.

If you opt for a custom GMS, you will get tailored features, greater scalability, and complete control over your system's data. Although ready-made solutions are cheaper initially, a custom system will align with your unique business processes.

Custom GMS may be a better solution for you in the following cases.

Unique Business Operations

If your fitness studio or gym runs on a niche model (e.g., *HIIT, CrossFit, martial arts, dance*), a custom system can better fit your workflows and generate specific analytics tailored to your predefined criteria.

Long-Term Growth

If your goal is to expand steadily, a custom platform will provide freedom - you can easily scale and adapt a custom solution to your future growth or shifts in your business strategy.

Data Control

If you rely heavily on member data, statistics, and payment analytics, a custom system will ensure that sensitive data is secured and aligned with relevant regulations. Having full ownership of your software today is a strategic advantage.

Integration with Existing Tools

If you already use certain software (e.g., *booking or accounting systems*), a custom solution will seamlessly integrate all the tools into a single platform.

Alternatives to GMS

Although a system tailored for your fitness business is the best choice, there are alternatives in case you do not need a complete GMS:

- **Other Management Software (Not Gym Related)** - You can manage your gym with software that is not fitness related. Some options include QuickBooks, NetSuite, or Trello offering features (e.g., *accounting, ERP (Enterprise Resource Planning)*) which can help business owners across diverse industries.
- **CRM or Marketing Automation Tools** - You can manage leads, send email/SMS, or create loyalty programs with tools like Mailchimp, ActiveCampaign, or specialized CRMs that can be tailored to fitness needs.
- **Standalone Booking or Scheduling Tools** - If you only need class booking, timetables, or reminders, you can use Calendly, Simply Studio, or Square Appointments to cover scheduling and class bookings.
- **Payment or Billing Systems** - In case you only need to manage payments, invoicing, or auto-renewal, you can use Stripe, PayPal, or local bank integration with simple spreadsheets.
- **Workout Progress Apps** - If you need to track member performance and progress rather than member check-ins or billing, apps like Fitbod and similar tracking apps will do the work.

- **Spreadsheets** – For very small studios, you can use Google Sheets, Excel, and Google Forms along with a simple booking link, creating a lightweight "*manual system*." You can further automate workflows via Zapier, Make.com, N8N, or other similar alternatives.
- **Virtual Assistant** – These can provide remote administrative assistance for your business and even help with advertising from anywhere in the world.

Benefits of a GMS for Your Gym Growth

If you want your fitness business to grow in today's competitive market, the right GMS will help you focus on what truly matters – **coaching, community building,** and **business growth**.

Let's list the benefits below.

Efficient Studio Management

With GMS, you can automate tasks like scheduling, payments, and member management and focus on running a business. Since all the data (*member, staff, operational*) is stored in a single platform, you can easily access and manage the data.

Enhanced Marketing and Sales

GMS will help you create targeted email/SMS campaigns for target demographics, attract new clients, and ensure timely follow-ups. Since you can simplify the process of online services (*classes, gear, supplements, etc.*), you can expand your reach and sales opportunities.

Better Financial Management

Integrated automated billing will help you with recurring payments and invoicing. You will be able to generate detailed financial reports for a complete overview over your revenue and expenses. Such insights will help you monitor your gym's overall financial health and better plan your future offerings.

Increased Member Retention

You will be able to monitor members' attendance and automatically send notifications or personalized offers to engage them further. Additionally, you will be able to collect members' feedback and act on it to improve both your services and member satisfaction.

Enhanced Compliance and Security

GMS comes with integrated security standards, ensuring all your data is securely stored and protected against breaches. Such a system will help you reduce legal risks and align with industry regulations.

If you implement a GMS, you can transform your fitness studio by improving member experiences, streamlining operations and finances, and obtaining actionable business insights.

The right GMS platform will enable you to focus on what truly matters - **your members**! With the right tools in place, you can focus on providing high-quality fitness services and stimulate your gym's growth.

The Best Gym Management System Examples

Today, you can find a variety of fitness software options designed for diverse fitness business models. If you struggle to find a perfect fit for your fitness business, check some of the most popular GMS examples, from complete solutions to specialized ones, designed for niche business models.

Each fitness software example below gives you a brief outline of

- **Key Features**
- **Pricing/Model** - *Subscription, per member, etc.*
- **Best For** - *For example, small studios, large gyms, boutique studios*

Complete Fitness Solutions

Let's check complete fitness solutions suitable for all business sizes and offerings that can scale from smaller businesses to multi-location gyms.

Mindbody

- Offers class bookings, payments, marketing, and customer relationship management (**CRM**). Automation tools help staff with detailed reports and analytics. The **Mindbody user app** helps businesses by listing them on a discovery network used by millions of fitness customers.
- A tiered subscription model - starter plan at **US$129-US$159 per month** while advanced tiers from **US$499 to US$699 per month**. Additional costs may apply (*onboarding, premium integrations, etc.*).
- Best for **medium** to **large fitness studios, boutique gyms, and wellness brands**. Ideal if you need to handle multiple staff members and class types.

Glofox (ABC Glofox)

- Glofox offers easy class scheduling, membership management, payments, and waitlist control. Includes engagement tools (*automated messaging, notifications, etc.*) and advanced analytics.
- A quote-based pricing model - entry level at around **US$100/month**. Depending on the size of your studio and add-ons, pricing ranges **US$250- US$600** while setup fees and add-on costs may apply.
- Best for **small to medium-sized boutique fitness studios** (e.g., *yoga, Pilates, CrossFit, pole dance*). Great if you operate at a single location or want to position your brand via a branded mobile app.

GymMaster

- Key features are managing memberships, attendance, and billing, along with class scheduling and online booking. Includes marketing tools, point-of-sale (POS) and inventory management, and detailed analytics. Suitable for **24/7 gyms** and fitness clubs that need reliable access control.

- GymMaster pricing depends on the number of members and hardware. The Foundation plan costs **US$89/month** for ~100 members, the Advanced **US$129/month** for ~400 members, and the Professional **US$209/month** for ~1300 members. Hardware like RFID readers or branded mobile apps come at additional cost.
- Best for gyms offering **around-the-clock access**, for **small to mid-sized** gyms or studios that want a comprehensive system. It suits gyms with **multiple services or locations**.

WellnessLiving

- Combines **scheduling, billing, POS, client,** and **staff management** - plus **reporting** along with **loyalty programs** - and **a video library**. Add-ons offer workout planning and leaderboards, and it supports both single- and multi-site operations.
- The **Starter plan** is **US$69/month**; the **Business plan** costs **US$199/month**, while the **BusinessPro plan** is **US$349/month**, with more features. Add-ons include a branded mobile app, website, virtual class tools, and SMS packages.
- Best for **small to large fitness businesses**, including boutique studios, and multi-location gyms.

Exercise.com

- Offers **class scheduling, staff and member management, check-ins, waivers/contracts,** and **reporting**. You can create custom workout plans and run online or hybrid training models. It supports ecommerce (*selling programs, memberships, digital workouts*), CRM, and marketing automation and multi-location.
- Custom pricing, which tends to be higher than simpler gym software tools. You will need to contact them for an exact quote.
- Best for **medium to large gyms**, or boutique fitness brands serious about their client experience. Great for scaling fitness businesses (***multiple locations***) or those who want to operate a hybrid model.

Figure 4-5 illustrates an example of a gym management system (GMS) interface, demonstrating key operational features used in fitness facility management.

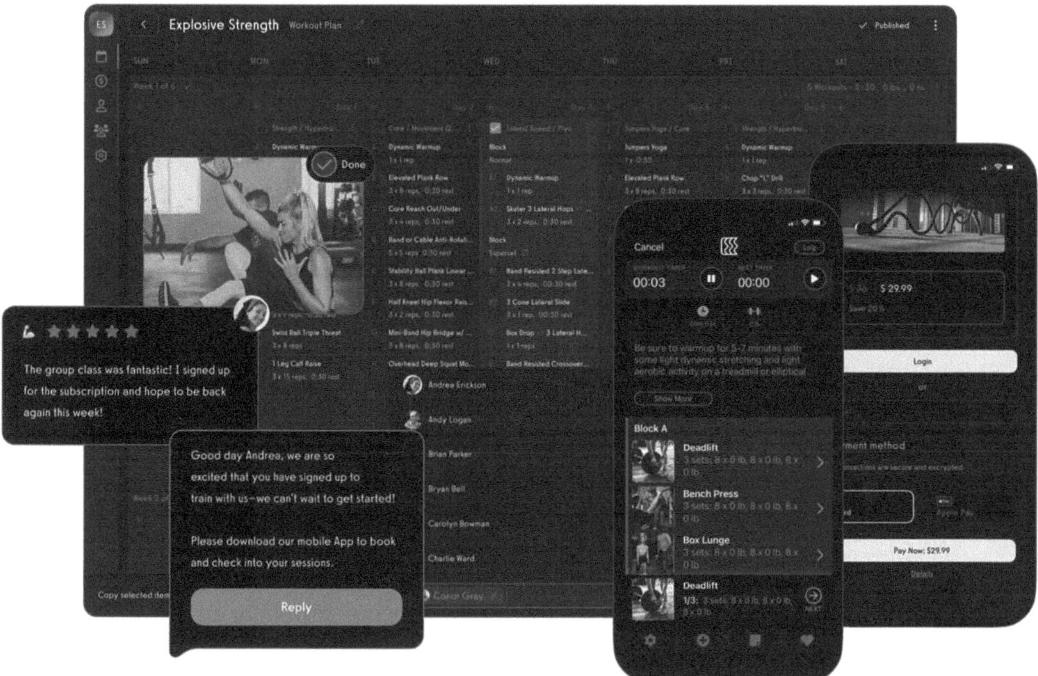

***Figure 4-5.** Example of a gym management system (GMS) interface from* `Exercise.com`*. Available at:* `http://exercise.com`

Gymdesk

- Manage **memberships, billing,** and **payments (+recurring), scheduling,** and **attendance tracking** via a simple interface. Core features for studios that don't need complex customizations.
- Tiers based on the number of **active members**. Micro plan (~50 active members) at **US$75/month,** Small (~100) at **US$100/month,** and Medium (~101–200) at **US$150/month.** Enterprise plan (~400 members) starts at **~US$200/month** + custom pricing beyond that. N**o long-term contracts, no hidden monthly fees, no cancellation fees** according to their site. Additional standard fees may incur (*Stripe, Square, etc., or SMS*), depending on the region.

- Best for **small to mid-sized** fitness businesses (*gyms, studios, martial arts schools, yoga/hybrid studios*) and for owners who want a **quick setup** and minimal training.

TeamUp

- Supports **scheduling, drop-ins, passes, and package-based attendance** including simple **reporting tools**. Offers robust marketing tools and all core features are included regardless of package.
- TeamUp pricing model is **based on the number of "active customers" per month**. A **free trial** is available, and then 0–100 active customers → **US$104/month**; 101–200 → **US$167/month,** etc. Confirm localization (*currency, language, payment gateways*) for operations in the United States, Central Europe, etc.
- Best for **small to medium-sized** studios that operate **class-based schedules** (*yoga, Pilates, group fitness, martial arts, pole dance*) and those wishing to minimize administrative overhead.

Virtuagym

- Combines **member management, automated billing, scheduling,** etc., workout plan creation, **nutrition planning, wearable integration,** and **advanced metrics**. Offers a web shop if you want to sell services or products in-app and more.
- The lack of fully transparent public pricing means you will typically get a custom quote. Check the contract terms carefully so as not to encounter any issues with payment vendors, etc.
- Best for **medium-sized to larger gyms** and those offering a **holistic solution,** those who **want** a **digital offering,** or studios prioritizing community building (*challenges, nutrition tracking, app usage*).

RhinoFit

- Budget-friendly, covering the essential management functions like **billing, scheduling, attendance, member communication,** etc. Offers extra features for martial arts schools (belt) and for gyms wishing 24/7 access control.
- A **"Start Up" plan** is free, the "Standard" plan is **US$57/month,** and 24/7 Access starts at **US$149/month** (*+hardware cost*) for larger/round-the-clock operations. Add-on costs include hardware, branded website services, EMV terminal add-ons, etc.
- Best for **small to medium-sized** gyms, studios, martial arts schools, or boot-camp-style operations. Several **add-ons** - payment processing fees are separate; regions outside the United States/ Canada may face different pricing or hardware logistics, etc.

Specialized Platforms for Niche Fitness

The list below lists solutions that serve specific niches like CrossFit, aerial sports, martial arts, personal trainers (PTs), etc. These solutions offer specific features like performance tracking, belt/progression, and class types like pole dance, yoga or solo coaching workflows, etc.

Everfit

- Program design and delivery, client scheduling and management (CRM), progress tracking and analytics, and client engagement tools for remote or hybrid coaching. Offers a branded mobile app, training content, and sale of coaching services and digital programs.
- A **free Starter plan for up to 5 clients**, and then it scales to a **Pro tier around US$16– US$19/month** for individual coaches and a **Studio tier around US$88– US$105/month** for larger coaching businesses, with options to add payment processing and automation as paid add-ons.
- For **personal trainers, online coaches, health and wellness professionals, and small studio owners** who deliver structured *programs*; for results-*driven coaching, programs, or challenges*; and for those who want to scale.

PushPress

- Member management, automated billing, scheduling, and check-ins. You can track performance through clear dashboards. There are add-ons like "*Train*" for workout tracking, etc., and a branded mobile app.
- A **Free plan** with higher transaction costs (*small gyms*). The **Pro plan** is **US$159/month** with reduced processing fees (*mid-size gyms*), while the **Max plan** costs **US$229/month** (*established gyms*) with multi-location support.
- Best for **small to mid-sized studios** focused on group classes like CrossFit, HIIT, or martial arts. It's perfect if you seek simple and scalable solutions.

Zen Planner

- Automates memberships, scheduling, and billing with performance tracking tools. Offers engagement tools via a branded mobile app, self-service check-in, belt/skill tracking (*useful for martial arts*), and integrations with platforms such as SugarWOD for workout.
- Has a tiered model based on the number of *active members*. The Basic Studio plan begins at around **US$99/month** for ~45 active members. Extras like website extension or a branded app come at additional cost.
- For gyms focusing on small group training and skill progression. Not suitable for large businesses with multiple locations.

As shown in Figure 4-6, gym management systems (GMS) are designed to be accessible across multiple devices, including mobile phones, tablets, and desktop computers.

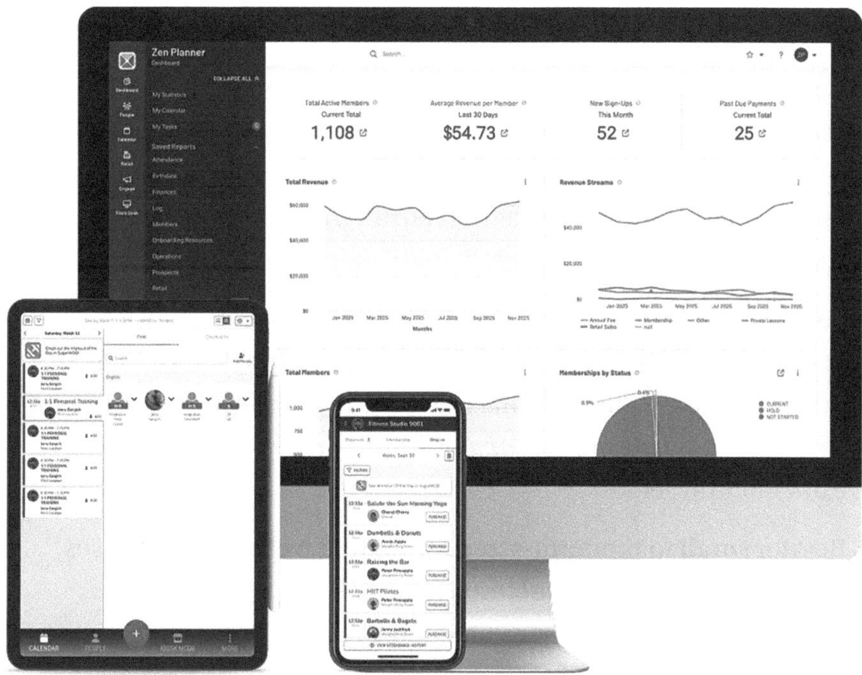

***Figure 4-6.** Example of a gym management system (GMS) interface from Zen Planner. Available at:* `https://zenplanner.com/`

WodGuru

- Combines **class/appointment scheduling, membership management, attendance tracking, online payments**, and **recurring billing** via Stripe. Includes POS for on-site sales, QR code and kiosk check-ins, automated reminders and rules, website embedding tools, and a member mobile app for self-service bookings and payments.
- **Pay-per-member** subscription model. Free plan for ~10 active members. The Pro plan is for 10+ active members, ranging from **US$49 to US$249**. Optional add-ons (e.g., *kiosk or QR access*) may incur additional fees.
- **Small to mid-sized** fitness businesses such as **boutique** studios, CrossFit boxes, yoga/pole dance studios, martial arts schools, etc. Well suited for **hybrid models** (group classes + PT).

Vagaro

- Combines **class scheduling, client profiles, payments,** and **marketing** in one system. Supports online booking, mobile apps for clients and staff, POS and retail sales, membership and inventory management, loyalty programs, reporting, and multi-location support. Offers branded apps, live streaming, etc., as add-ons.
- Subscription model based on the number of users. Pricing starts at **US$30/month for one user**, increasing by **US$10/month per additional user**. International pricing varies by region and optional add-ons (*POS hardware, branded app, live streaming*) may bring extra monthly fees.
- Best for **small to medium-sized** fitness and **wellness** businesses (*boutique studios, personal trainers, yoga/Pilates studios*). Less suitable for large gym chains or enterprises.

Teep Software

- Supports **membership management, automated renewals** and **billing, class bookings, lead management, and built-in reporting** to track revenue, etc. Includes specific tools such as martial arts belt/progression tracking, with add-ons like *in-app shopping platform, video courses, a custom mobile app,* and *website integration* listed as upcoming.
- Subscription-based model. The Professional plan starts at **US$129/month**, with a lower **Founders plan around US$69.99/month** available under certain conditions. No setup fees and no long-term contracts.
- Best for **single-location boutique** fitness businesses and owners who value community engagement. Less ideal for multi-location chains or advanced integrations.

SimpleGym

- Includes **membership management, automated billing** and **payments**, attendance tracking with check-in, and belt/rank tracking for martial arts schools. Additional tools available for more detailed analytics.
- Highly flexible pricing model. A **Free plan** with **US$0 monthly fee** + processing premium (+1%). For large businesses, a **Pro plan** is around **US$149/month**, removing the extra processing markup. Core features are available on the free tier.
- Best for **small to mid-sized** gyms, **boutique** studios, **personal trainers**, and businesses focused on memberships. Less suitable for large multi-location chains or requiring customized workflows.

Wodify

- Includes **class scheduling, membership management, automated billing, integrated payments,** and **attendance tracking**. Community and performance tools allow users to log workouts, track personal records, view leaderboards, and compare results. Add-ons include staff/member mobile apps, lead management, marketing tools, POS integration, etc.
- Subscription-based, priced per location, and feature tier. Plans start around **US$100/month per location** for the Essentials plan, with higher tiers (*e.g., Accelerate, Ultimate*). Optional add-ons and onboarding fees may apply.
- Best for **CrossFit boxes**, functional fitness gyms, HIIT and boot camp studios, and **boutique** gyms. Ideal for businesses that want to motivate members through data, challenges, and measurable results.

Class-Centered Fitness Platforms

Class-centered platforms are simple fitness solutions built ***around classes*** – a clear schedule, easy booking, and straightforward payment and attendance tracking. **The class is the core unit** (*schedule it, sell it, track attendance*) while other features are less important.

Punchpass

- Offers class scheduling, online booking, pass and membership sales, and basic client communications. Includes features like waitlists, class reminders, and private sessions. You can also offer live or virtual classes through Zoom and embed your schedule on your website.
- The basic plan at **US$49/month**, the mid-tier plan ~**US$99/month**, and the top tier plan ~**US$149/month**, which includes advanced automation. All plans are month-to-month with no long-term contracts.
- Best for small to medium fitness and specialty studios (*e.g., pole, yoga, barre*) that want a user-friendly schedule and pass system.

Figure 4-7 illustrates a gym management system (GMS) interface from Punchpass, highlighting scheduling and class management functionality.

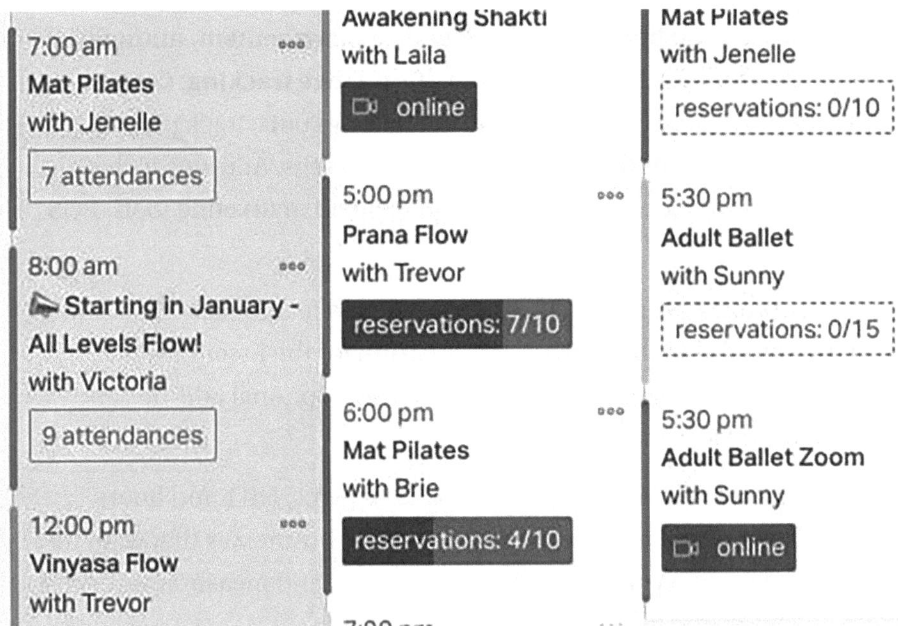

Figure 4-7. *Example of a gym management system (GMS) interface from Punchpass. Available at:* `https://punchpass.com/features/reports-and-analytics/`

Gymcatch

- Simple class and appointment scheduling with unlimited bookings, online payment integration (Stripe), client profiles, event scheduling, and bundles of passes. Supports livestream and on-demand classes and you can add referral marketing or custom waivers for a small extra monthly cost.
- Doesn't publicly list pricing but offers a free trial and plans that scale with added features, typically billed monthly with no lock-in.
- Best for boutique studios and personal trainers who want flexible class booking and client engagement, particularly studios with a mix of in-person and online classes.

Momoyoga

- For any studio that needs booking, payments, and client management. Includes **online booking** and cancellation windows, waitlists, membership and pass options, automated messaging, Zoom integration, and a mobile app for clients.
- A free plan (a small platform fee on payments), then Standard (~**€29/month**), and a Plus (~**€59/month**) plan. All plans are billed monthly or annually and without long-term contracts.
- Best for small studios and independent trainers looking for an affordable system and those focused on regular classes and community engagement.

Choosing the appropriate gym management system (GMS) will directly influence the efficiency and viability of your fitness business. The right platform will improve the overall client experience and provide actionable data to support your further growth.

While complete solutions like GymMaster and Mindbody offer robust management and marketing capabilities suited to a broad range of studios, specialized platforms such as Zen Planner or Glofox cater to niche segments with tailored functionalities. Simple software like Punchpass or Gymcatch focus only on managing classes efficiently. Each of these systems provides specific advantages depending on your business model, operational scale, and growth objectives.

Finally, choose GMS as per your own studio's unique needs, your budget, and long-term goals. Implementing the right system will enable you to streamline business operations and devote more time to high-quality training experiences and sustainable business growth.

4.3 Mobile Apps – Staff App vs. Client App

Gym management software (GMS) commonly provides two separate mobile applications, one for **staff** or **administrators** and the other for **members**. Although these apps are integrated within the same system, they are designed for different purposes and user roles.

The **member app** serves as a personalized interface for users to view membership details, class schedules, manage payments, and receive any upcoming studio announcements. Members can book or cancel classes, renew membership, follow studio news, and monitor their personal progress, creating motivating training experience.

The **staff app** helps trainers and administrators by consolidating business operations in a single platform. Trainers can view assigned classes, confirm attendance, and track performance directly from their mobile phones. They can also manage shifts, monitor studio availability, and access member profiles. Features like instant messaging and notifications facilitate efficient communication while integrated payroll allows staff to review their completed sessions and pay summaries.

Today, having both a staff app and a customized member app will bring significant benefits from saving time to driving client engagement, making these tools invaluable assets.

Staff App vs. Client App: What's the Difference?

The mobile applications enable smooth interaction between members, trainers, and administrators, and although a part of the same system, they are designed for entirely different purposes.

Let's check the key functional differences between staff and member applications.

Primary Function

- The **staff app** is for professionals, enabling them to handle administrative tasks (e.g., *checking attendance, managing schedules, tracking client progress, processing payments, communicating internally*) in real time. The goal is to ensure smooth coordination between all departments within the gym or studio.
- The **member app** is all about clients' experience. It provides members with 24/7 access to core services such as booking classes, checking schedules, managing payments, and tracking attendance/progress. By offering easy communication features, you improve user engagement, retention, and overall satisfaction.

Access Level and Permissions

- The **staff** app provides permission-based access - admins can monitor member accounts, edit schedules, and update system settings while trainers can only see member data, class schedules, or performance logs. With strict access settings, you will protect sensitive data and allow only authorized access.
- **Member** apps allow clients to manage their profiles, view classes, and personal progress. They can update certain profile information like contact details but cannot access or edit administrative data.

Check-In Control

- **Staff** can access the app from anywhere, allowing manual entry or validating class attendance.
- The **member** app offers a digital check-in system (e.g., *QR code, barcode*) for members to verify their membership or class booking, improving contactless access control.

Communication and Messaging

- The **staff** can communicate with members and send news, announcements, or even push notifications for member milestones or achievements. Managers can send updates or event notifications directly from the app.
- The **member** app acts as a two-way communication tool, to confirm bookings, ask questions, and more. Member apps usually include community hubs where users can interact or participate in challenges.

Scheduling and Bookings

- The **staff** app provides control over the class calendar, where staff can add classes, assign instructors, manage substitutions, and define capacity limits in real time. It provides a live overview, enabling staff to check in members or mark absences directly from the app.
- The **member** app allows users to book or cancel the classes, browse, and join waitlists. They can filter content by categories (*trainer, class type, or time*) while push notifications confirm any changes in the system, like rescheduling and similar.

Payments and Billing

- The **staff** app handles payments via POS, manages membership, issues refunds, views payment history, etc. You can also generate daily sales reports or revenue dashboards for financial insights.
- The **member** app provides a self-service to purchase class packages or single sessions, manage membership renewals, and view past transactions. Receipts are sent automatically via email or app.

Performance Tracking

- The **staff** app generates business performance reports and client analytics, from attendance to revenue summaries and staff productivity. Trainers can review progress data to adapt sessions or track class engagement over time.

- The **member** app focuses on user metrics like workout stats, personal records, nutrition logs, etc. Some apps display progress via graphs, improving retention.

Security and Data Handling

- The **staff** app provides access with multi-factor authentication, role-based access, or encrypted connection and complies with data privacy regulations like GDPR and HIPAA where necessary.
- The **member** app stores only personal and fitness data relevant to the user. The system security protects payment data while members can manage consent for data sharing and notifications.

Marketing and Engagement

- The **staff** app tracks marketing campaigns like referral or loyalty programs and promotions. Staff can monitor campaign performance, re-engage leads with promotional offers, or filter audiences by pre-set parameters.
- **Members** receive promotional messages, loyalty rewards, or referral invitations via their app. They can share achievements, reviews, or social posts that promote your gym.

Integrations and Automation

- The **staff** app integrates with tools like CRM, accounting software (e.g., *QuickBooks*), marketing software (e.g., *MailChimp, HubSpot*), or payment systems (e.g., *Stripe, PayPal*). These help you automate workflows in certain cases like "*send follow-up message if a member misses 3 classes*," etc.
- The **member** app syncs wearable devices (e.g., *Fitbit, Garmin*), nutrition trackers, or social media for easy sharing. Automation supports reminders, progress updates, and rewards.

Key Functional Differences – Staff vs. Member App

As shown in Table 4-1, staff and member fitness applications differ significantly in terms of functionality, access level, and operational features.

Table 4-1. *Key functional differences between staff and member fitness mobile applications. Source: Created by the author*

STAFF VS MEMBER FITNESS MOBILE APPLICATION

FEATURES	STAFF APP	MEMBER APP
PRIMARY USER	TRAINERS, ADMINISTRATORS, AND OWNERS	MEMBERS AND CLIENTS
CORE FUNCTION	MANAGEMENT AND OPERATIONAL INTERFACE	SELF-SERVICE APP FOR CLASS BOOKING, PAYMENTS, AND COMMUNICATION
ACCESS LEVEL	BROADER ACCESS + CLASS ROSTERS, PAYMENTS & MEMBER DETAILS	LIMITED TO PERSONAL DATA AND BOOKINGS
COMMUNICATION TOOLS	INTERNAL MESSAGING, TASK ASSIGNMENTS, AND CLIENT COMMUNICATION	NOTIFICATIONS, EMAILS, AND CHAT SUPPORT
SCHEDULING	CREATE, EDIT, AND MONITOR SCHEDULES	VIEW AND BOOK AVAILABLE CLASSES
DATA HANDLING	MONITORS ALL MEMBER ACTIVITIES AND ANALYTICS	TRACKS PERSONAL ATTENDANCE AND PROGRESS
PAYMENTS	PROCESS PAYMENTS, ISSUE REFUNDS, MANAGE INVOICES	PAY FOR MEMBERSHIPS, RENEW PLANS
SECURITY AND PERMISSIONS	ROLE-BASED ACCESS CONTROL DEPENDING ON STAFF ROLE	RESTRICTED TO PERSONAL ACCOUNT

In short, the **member app** is about convenience and engagement, while the **staff app** is about control and coordination. Together, they create a consolidated digital ecosystem where both sides interact smoothly, improving both user satisfaction and operational performance.

Benefits of a Staff App for Your Business

A staff app will turn your gym staff into a coordinated team with benefits like

Easy Access - Instant access to training schedules, substitutions, and upcoming classes. All trainers know their agenda, without numerous spreadsheets or errors.

Reduced Errors - Automated schedules, attendance tracking, and payroll data eliminate manual work and reduce last-minute issues.

Improved Communication - Staff receive important information via app in real time (*announcements, schedule changes, etc.*), preventing misunderstandings.

Performance and Attendance Tracking - Trainers can track class attendance, cancellations, and client engagement, while admins obtain performance data without micromanaging.

Quality Consistency - With shared notes, class templates, and studio standards, every trainer will deliver a quality experience, hence improving your brand recognition.

Professional Accountability - With clear roles, trainers can schedule hours and responsibilities smoothly, supporting a professional culture.

Scalability - As your business grows, the staff app helps keep operations structured. In case of more instructors and more classes, you will have the same level of control without operational burden.

Benefits of a Client App for Your Business

A member app will provide your clients a smoother and more engaging experience.

Stronger Client Engagement - The app keeps members connected to your studio since easy access to schedules, bookings, and progress tracking increases consistency and reduces missed classes.

Improved Retention - Clients can see their attendance, progress rewards, or milestones and stay more committed. Simple rescheduling and automated reminders reduce drop-offs and last-minute cancellations.

Premium Brand Experience - A branded client app improves your gym's reputation, builds trust, and positions your business alongside top-tier fitness brands.

Operational Efficiency - Self-booking, automated payments, confirmations, and cancellations significantly reduce administrative work. This frees up time for coaching, programming, and scaling the business.

Communication Hub - All gym communication is in one place. Push notifications ensure clients receive important updates instantly, eliminating confusion.

Data-Driven Strategy - With clear insights into attendance patterns, popular classes, and engagement levels, you can optimize schedules, pricing, and offers based on real data.

Increased Revenue Opportunities - Clients will more likely opt for add-ons when offered relevant content - you can offer workshops, challenges, private sessions, and upgrades directly in the app.

Stronger Community - The app helps increase the feeling of loyalty through shared challenges, announcements, and studio milestones. A sense of community turns clients into loyal and long-term members.

If you wish to streamline your fitness business and make your gym more accessible on the go in today's modern world, provide a dedicated fitness app, both for your staff and your clients.

4.4 Personal Coaching

Once you earn your PT certificate (the United States or Europe), the first thing is to do your research on your **ideal** client; check what other PTs offer and to whom, meaning to what type of users. Check on marketing tools you can use to help you find your clients whether via social media, local marketing outreach, or word of mouth.

As a personal trainer (PT), you can choose your business model from being a fitness instructor in a gym or launching your own PT business online. Once you decide how to position yourself, keep in mind that there are many opportunities which can help you to grow your business or reputation.

As a personal trainer (PT), you need to be efficient, and the right software will help you manage your clients and keep your business running smoothly. However, with so many different PT software options available, you will have to choose the best one for your specific needs.

Let's explore what personal business software is, the key features, and how it can benefit your clients.

What Is Personal Training Software?

Personal training (PT) software helps personal trainers and very small studios manage daily activities from administrative tasks, bookings, and client management to payment processing.

The software is a centralized database that allows you to streamline repetitive and time-consuming tasks. Since it is a cloud-based solution, your users can access the software from anywhere and confirm their schedules or track progress.

A PT software is a tool intended primarily for coaches and personal trainers as it automates daily tasks like

- **Communication** – From client check-ins and progress to ability to create personalized workouts or send suggested workout videos. Additionally, you can send reminders to clients or rewards each time they complete a certain fitness goal.
- **Client Management** – It can help automate tasks like sign-up, creating profiles, or managing assessments. For example, after a session, you can log the fitness status of your client, ensuring the training program is ideal for them.

- **Integrations** – PT software is easily integrated into your website or social media account, so you can post content on your website and social media pages. You can create blog posts about fitness related topics or update your coaching schedule on your website or social media page.

Check the key features of effective personal training (PT) software in Figure 4-8.

Figure 4-8. *Key features of effective personal training software, Smart Health Clubs (2025). Five key features to look for in personal training software. Available at:* `https://smarthealthclubs.com/blog/5-key-features-to-look-for-in-personal-training-software/`

Benefits of PT software

For personal trainers, this type of software is a complete tech tool that facilitates managing clients.

Saves Time

Fitness software reduces manual work - you can create workout plans with templates and exercise libraries, automate client check-ins, and set reminders for progress updates or missed workouts. You will be able to focus on the quality of your coaching and running your business.

Helps Grow Your Business

Automation will allow you to manage more clients at the same time, without impacting the quality of your coaching. You can offer hybrid or online coaching, sell pre-made training programs, and monthly memberships, thus creating additional revenue streams.

Improves Client Organization

All client information (*goals, workouts, injuries, measurements, habits, etc.*) is neatly organized in this centralized system, reducing the risk of miscommunication or errors. By staying organized, you ensure a smoother experience for each client.

Better Results for Clients

PT software helps your clients get better results because their plans are structured. They can track their workouts, check progress charts, and stay consistent through habit tracking. "*Seeing*" the improvement keeps them motivated and increases their overall satisfaction.

Clear Communication

In-app messaging facilitates communication with clients - they can send videos for checks, and trainers can respond with feedback, corrections, or encouragement. This steady communication boosts engagement, helping clients stay on track.

Simple Payments and Scheduling

Most software integrates billing tools that handle payments, subscriptions, and invoices automatically. You can set up reminders for renewals and missed payments, while built-in features help you manage sessions and availability more efficiently.

Recognizable Brand

Many platforms allow you to customize the experience with your own logo, brand colors, or even a fully branded app. This creates a more personalized feel and sets you apart from trainers that use basic spreadsheets or messaging apps. Strong branding builds trust and builds on the value of your coaching services.

Moving your personal training business online opens huge opportunities for growth. Your clients can join your classes from anywhere in the world, so even when they are on vacation or traveling for work, they can stay consistent with their workouts.

It also allows you to market yourself far beyond your local area. With online personal training becoming increasingly popular, you are no longer restricted to finding clients locally - your potential reach is global.

The Best Apps for Personal Trainers

When selecting PT software, think of aspects such as ***your coaching style, target clients, and your specific business needs*** to choose the platform that best aligns with your goals.

Each example below includes a quick overview of

- **Key Features** - What the software does best
- **Pricing** - Cost or model (e.g., *subscription, per member*)
- **Best For** - Who benefits most (e.g., *personal trainers, small studios*)

The platforms listed below are mostly **complete PT solutions**.

Virtuagym

- Offers workouts, nutrition plans, wearable integration, progress tracking, and custom branding as well as membership management and an automated online store. **Virtuagym's free coaching app** features personalized coaching, nutrition solutions, and tracking tools to help users reach their fitness goals.
- Subscription-based; usually starts around **US$50/month**.
- For fitness studios, gyms, or coaches wanting a fully branded, all-in-one coaching solution.

TrueCoach

- Offers robust client engagement tools, streamlines workflow, and enhances client communication. Trainers can assign custom workout plans, track client progress, and integrate with wearable apps. The analytics dashboard helps optimize training results.
- Subscription-based; starts around **US$50/month** for a small number of clients, scaling with more clients.
- For independent PTs or small coaching businesses who want to improve client engagement and data-driven training.

PT Minder

- Client management, bookings, payments, progress tracking, and integration with marketing platforms. Clients can self-manage bookings and view workouts. Integration with marketing platforms such as Mailchimp and Facebook, etc.
- Subscription-based; starts at around **US$29/month**.
- For trainers or small studios who want a user-friendly platform combining scheduling, client management, and marketing.

Total Coaching

- Exercise and nutrition management with a library of 1000+ exercises and nutritional data for 25,000+ food. Offers custom questionnaires, progress graphs, private messaging, and real-time analysis for adjusting clients' diet.
- Subscription-based; starts around **US$39/month**.
- For online personal trainers who want a highly customizable platform with nutrition and exercise tracking.

Workout Labs

- Custom workouts, progress monitoring, nutrition tracking, and client notes. Easy sharing via email or text.
- Subscription-based; pricing starts around **US$10-US$15/month**.
- For independent trainers or small teams who want a platform for workout creation and client tracking.

Just Coach

- Client profiles, appointment scheduling, workout and payment tracking, secure data storage, and messaging. Easy setup and management.
- Subscription model; starts around **US$10/month**.
- For trainers looking for a cost-effective platform for managing client schedules and data.

PT Distinction

- Offers extensive customization of workouts, nutrition plans, and client portals. Supports automated communication and branded app experiences.
- Subscription model, usually starting around **US$30/month**.
- For trainers who want highly tailored programs and value branding and those who want to tailor their services to individual client needs.

Trainerfu

- Branded app experience, custom workouts, progress tracking, and client messaging. Allows trainers to maintain their brand identity while offering clients a consistent training experience.
- Subscription-based; pricing starts at **US$19/month**.
- For personal trainers or small studios seeking a branded app to engage clients online.

FitBudd

- Supports hybrid coaching with both online and in-person sessions, progress tracking, and workout programming, beneficial for trainers managing diverse client schedules.
- Subscription model; typically starts around **US$19-US$29/month**.
- Personal trainers managing a mix of online and face-to-face clients.

WodGuru

- Designed for CrossFit and functional training, including workout logging, class scheduling, and performance tracking. Specialized for high-intensity programs.
- Subscription-based; usually starts near **US$20/month**.
- CrossFit gyms, functional training studios, and coaches specializing in high-intensity programs.

My PT Hub

- Workout creation, client management, progress tracking, and payment processing. Integrates nutrition and workout plans in one platform.
- Starts around **US$12/month** for a smaller number of clients and scales with larger client bases.
- Personal trainers or small teams who want a complete solution for managing clients and payments.

The next section lists several platforms that are **not complete PT platforms** - they handle **scheduling, payments, or nutrition tracking**, but lack workout programming or full client management features.

Acuity Scheduling

- Online appointment booking, automated reminders, payment processing, and real-time calendar management.

- Subscription model; starts at **US$15/month**.
- For personal trainers, small studios, or gyms that need efficient appointment and client scheduling.

MyFitnessPal

- Tracks client diet, workout, weight changes, and nutrition; barcode scanner for food products and social sharing included. Provides detailed analytics on health and fitness goals and an article library on healthy eating and recipes.
- Free basic version while premium upgrades start around **US$10/month**.
- Fitness coaches and clients who want detailed nutritional and exercise tracking.

Vagaro

- Scheduling, payments, client database, email/text marketing, personalized newsletters and alerts via email or SMS, and analytics. Easy to manage clients and setup and use on any device.
- Subscription-based; starts at **US$25/month**.
- For personal trainers, gyms, and studios needing a comprehensive business management tool.

If your goal is **full PT management** or to **run your PT business solo** (*online or hybrid*) and serve clients completely with workouts, nutrition, tracking, payments, and communication, focus on complete fitness platform examples. If you just need **supplementary tools** (*scheduling, payment collection, nutrition tracking*) or you already have a workout program, then Acuity, MyFitnessPal, Vagaro, and similar tools can be a helpful add-on.

Many coaches find the best results by **combining** a full PT tool with complementary ones, depending on their specific needs (e.g., *scheduling + nutrition + payments + program delivery*).

4.5 Examples of Gym Management System

Here is a consolidated list of **all gym management system (GMS) platforms mentioned in this chapter.** For more details on each software, check sections "The Best Gym Management System Examples" and "The Best Apps for Personal Trainers."

Mindbody - A large-scale fitness and wellness management platform with robust scheduling, payments, CRM, automation, and a large consumer discovery marketplace

Glofox (ABC Glofox) - A boutique-focused gym software offering branded mobile apps, memberships, class booking, and marketing automation for studios

GymMaster - Gym management software known for strong 24/7 access control, membership management, billing, and hardware integrations

WellnessLiving - An all-in-one platform combining scheduling, billing, POS, marketing automation, loyalty programs, and multi-location management

Exercise.com - A high-end, white-label fitness platform for gyms and studios offering custom-branded apps, training delivery, CRM, and hybrid/online models

Gymdesk - A simple, affordable gym management system focused on memberships, billing, scheduling, and CRM for small to mid-sized studios

TeamUp - Class-based studio software emphasizing flexible memberships, clean scheduling, and transparent pricing based on active customers

Virtuagym - A holistic fitness platform combining gym management with workout planning, nutrition tracking, wearables, and community features

RhinoFit - A budget-friendly gym management solution offering essential tools like billing, attendance, POS, and optional 24/7 access control

Everfit - A coaching platform that helps fitness business owners manage clients, deliver personalized training and nutrition plans, and track progress all in one place

PushPress - A scalable gym management platform for group-based gyms, offering billing, scheduling, check-ins, and optional training modules

Zen Planner - Software built for CrossFit, martial arts, and niche gyms with strong membership automation, skill tracking, and branded apps

WodGuru - A pay-per-member gym management system focused on simplicity, automation, class booking, and affordability for small studios

Vagaro - A booking-first business management platform widely used in wellness and fitness for scheduling, payments, POS, and marketing

Teep Software - A boutique and martial-arts-focused platform offering memberships, billing, scheduling, and community-oriented growth tools

SimpleGym - A low-cost, fast-setup gym management system with billing automation, attendance tracking, waivers, and martial arts features

Wodify - A specialist platform for CrossFit and performance-based gyms focused on WOD (Workout of the Day) tracking, leaderboards, billing, and community engagement

Punchpass - A lightweight class-pass and scheduling tool popular with yoga, dance, and specialty studios

Gymcatch - A simple booking and management platform that helps fitness business owners schedule classes, handle payments, and manage clients

Momoyoga - A simple booking platform that helps yoga and boutique fitness studio owners schedule classes, accept payments, and automate client bookings in one place

TrueCoach – A trainer-focused coaching app designed for assigning workouts, tracking progress, integrating wearables, and maintaining strong client communication

PT Minder – A user-friendly system that blends client management, scheduling, payments, workout access, and marketing integrations in one platform

Total Coaching – A highly customizable online coaching platform with extensive exercise and nutrition databases, real-time analysis, and client messaging

Workout Labs – A lightweight tool for coaches to create workouts, track progress, manage notes, and share programs easily with clients

Just Coach – A simple, low-cost platform for managing client profiles, scheduling, workouts, payments, and secure communication

PT Distinction – A branding-driven coaching platform offering deep customization of workouts, nutrition plans, automation, and client portals

Trainerfu – A branded coaching app that enables trainers to deliver workouts, track progress, and communicate with clients under their own brand

FitBudd – A hybrid coaching platform designed to manage both online and in-person training with scheduling, workouts, and progress tracking

WodGuru – A functional fitness and CrossFit-oriented platform supporting workout logging, class scheduling, and performance tracking

My PT Hub – Complete personal training platform for workouts, nutrition, client management, progress tracking, and payments

Acuity Scheduling – An online appointment scheduling tool with automated reminders, payments, and real-time calendar management

MyFitnessPal - A widely used nutrition and fitness tracking app offering calorie logging, exercise tracking, analytics, and food databases

Vagaro - A business management platform for fitness and wellness providers covering scheduling, payments, marketing, and client management

Bonus – Best Ways to Monetize a Fitness App

Modern technologies create new opportunities for your fitness business, but the monetization model you choose will determine how much revenue it will generate. Before choosing a revenue strategy, understand the context of your business, your products, and users. The right revenue model does not depend just on what you offer but also on how you offer it, when, and to whom.

Key Factors to Consider

- **App Type and Usage Scenario** - Different apps do not monetize the same way. Daily used apps can profit from subscriptions while goal-based apps capitalize the best from one-time purchases or challenges. Define what type of app matches your business and determine the monetization model that supports your goals.
- **Audience Motivation** - Define your target audience and analyze the demographics: *Are your users price-conscious or value-oriented? Do they want long-term results or short-term try-outs?* Collecting user feedback can also be a great source of information.
- **Market Landscape and Expectations** - Study your competitors and discover what price users expect to pay for similar services. Define your offer and discover similarities or gaps which you can cover in case other competitors did not.

Let's check some monetization ideas for you that look the most promising in today's market:

1. **Subscription-Based Services** - Still popular in the fitness industry. It involves membership fees for continued access to the offered content.
2. **One-Time Purchase Workout Plans** - Offer workout plans as individual purchases or exclusive content on a paid basis.
3. **Fitness Classes** - Charge for access to online fitness classes or personal training.
4. **Personal Training Packages** - Sell packages of personal training sessions for a fixed fee.
5. **In-App Purchases** - Offer premium content or features for an additional cost.
6. **Ecommerce Shop** - Sell products (*gear/supplements*) directly from the app.
7. **Nutrition Plans** - Sell personalized nutrition plans for healthy eating and meal preparation + workout content.
8. **Sponsored Challenges** - Create fitness challenges sponsored by other similar or relevant businesses.
9. **Premium Subscriptions** - Offer an upgraded subscription level with additional perks.
10. **Virtual Coaching** - Charge a fee for personalized, individual virtual coaching sessions.
11. **Master Classes** - Host master classes or workshops on a specific fitness topic for a certain fee.
12. **Certification Programs** - Specialized training and certification programs for a fee.
13. **Exclusive Community Access** - Charge for access to a members-only online community.
14. **Paid Fitness Events** - Host virtual fitness events or webinars that participants pay to join.

15. **Webinars and Seminars** - Sell tickets for online educational fitness webinars.
16. **Fitness Books** - Write and sell your own books or eBooks on relevant topics.
17. **Licensed Content** - License your fitness content to other platforms or businesses.
18. **Brand Partnerships** - Partner with other relevant brands for joint marketing efforts.
19. **Advertising** - Host sponsored content or display ads from relevant businesses.
20. **Affiliate Marketing** - Earn commissions by recommending related products and receiving a percentage of each sale generated through your app.
21. **Data Monetization** - If your users consent, you can offer anonymized data to market researchers.
22. **Donations** - Accept donations from satisfied users who wish to support your platform.
23. **Rent Ad Space** - If you have a high traffic volume, you can rent ad space in your app.

How to Appeal to Fitness Consumers?

Let's outline a few key steps to follow to appeal to fitness consumers from a marketing standpoint:

- **Focus on Personalization** - Promote workouts tailored to users' individual needs and preferences. You can stand out in the market by offering personalized workouts based on data insights or customization options allowing users choose exercises, equipment, and intensity levels.
- **Focus on Technology** - Many people today use wearable technology and fitness apps. You should look for ways to integrate these technologies into your offerings and highlight how these can improve

workout experience for users, like tracking progress or connecting users with virtual trainers.

- **Focus on Diversity and Inclusivity** – Younger generations think about social and environmental issues. Promote diversity and inclusivity in your ads and highlight your commitment to sustainability or social responsibility.
- **Focus on Creating a Community** – Focus on elements of your offerings that create a sense of community. You can achieve this by organizing events or workshops, offering group workout classes, or creating online forums where users can connect and share tips.

In conclusion, fitness companies should focus on offering a personalized tech-driven workout experience that meets specific needs and preferences of the target demographic. If you emphasize these values, you can position yourself as a leader in a rapidly evolving industry and attract a loyal audience of fitness enthusiasts.

Figure 4-9 illustrates three practical strategies that fitness businesses can apply immediately to grow smarter.

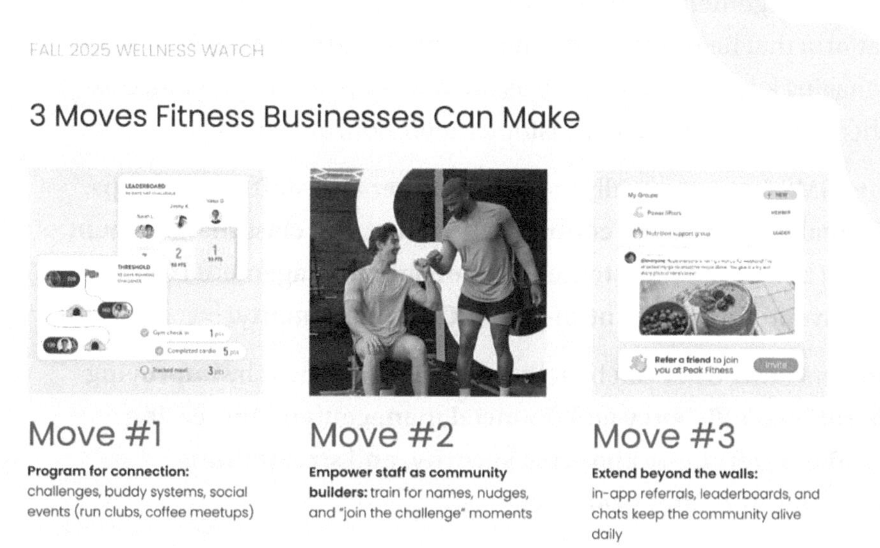

Figure 4-9. *Three strategic moves for fitness businesses. Source: ABC Fitness Wellness Watch Fall 2025. Available at: abcfitness.com*

The Way Forward for Fitness Leaders – Tips

- Start small and simple.
- Begin with accessible solutions like scheduling software or member apps to see immediate benefits.
- Leverage data and use analytics to understand member behavior and identify trends for more informed decisions.
- Partner with experts and collaborate with digital specialists to create a roadmap tailored to your specific business goals (*increase member acquisition or retention, introduce new offers, grow your business in terms of profit or community, etc.*).
- Focus on outcomes and prioritize tools that directly impact revenue and member satisfaction to ensure a clear ROI.

4.6 Key Takeaways

- **Gym management system (GMS)** is typically a cloud-based SaaS platform that helps fitness businesses run more efficiently by managing key operations such as membership administration, class scheduling, sales tracking, customer retention, and analytics.
- Core GMS features usually include **member and staff mobile apps, attendance and access control, scheduling and class management, billing and payroll, customer relationship management (CRM), and inventory with point-of-sale (POS) functionality**.
- Implementing GMS can benefit your fitness business by **improving operational efficiency and financial management, increasing member retention, enhancing security, and streamlining marketing and sales processes**.
- Many GMS provide two separate mobile applications, a **staff/ administrator app** for managing business operations and a **member app** that allows users to manage bookings, memberships, and track their fitness progress.

- Personal training (PT) software helps personal trainers and very small studios manage daily operations such as client administration, scheduling, and payment processing. These tools save time, improve client management, and allow you to scale your business beyond the local area.
- When choosing a revenue model for your fitness app, review the type of your business (e.g., *subscriptions, online training*), your products, and users. This includes identifying the app type that best fits the business, selecting an appropriate monetization model, and defining the target audience through demographic research. Study your competitors to identify common practices, discover market gaps, and generate ideas for new services or features that differentiate your offering.
- If you wish to appeal to modern consumers, focus on personalization, technology integration, and building a diverse, inclusive community.

CHAPTER 5

For Fitness Enthusiasts

Chapter 5 brings all the fun for fitness enthusiasts – whether you are a beginner or an experienced athlete, you will discover how to track your performance with innovative apps, use connected devices like fitness trackers or smartwatches, stay motivated by joining online communities, improve your recovery with modern techniques like app-assisted meditation, and more.

5.1 Age of Online Fitness – What Fitness Lovers Want from Their Workout?

Before the pandemic, fitness as an online business was already mainstream, driven by wearables and Instagram culture where digital fitness was a *supplement* to traditional gyms. The pandemic period accelerated the entire industry as lockdowns forced gyms to close their physical facilities and shift businesses online. This period was a true turning point for the fitness industry – gyms discovered new opportunities with online training and clients discovered that online training saves time, offers flexibility to train anywhere, and can be personalized to their specific needs.

After COVID, many fitness users went back to gyms but kept their digital habits. Online training remained popular, especially among younger generations who value flexibility, personalization, and technology-driven fitness. Younger generations are redefining the fitness industry as they seek out alternative training options that better align with their preferences and values.

As a result, a new generation of fitness fans want flexibility, digital integration, and social connection in their workouts. This does not include only *in-person* or *online* training, but also *mental* and *holistic wellness* as well as group experiences that offer a strong sense of community.

M. Dakić, *When Fitness Goes Tech*, https://doi.org/10.1007/979-8-8688-2457-9_5

Modern fitness has evolved in response to the key expectations of the fitness fans, such as

- **Flexibility and Convenience** - Because of tight schedules, users value flexibility and are more likely to choose a hybrid model that blends gym visits with on-demand or live-streamed digital workouts.
- **Digital Integration** - Users want seamless technology throughout their fitness journey, including apps for tracking, booking, and accessing virtual coaching.
- **Social Connection** - Users like supportive group classes, which can provide motivation, a sense of community, and the opportunity to socially connect with others.
- **Holistic Wellness** - Users prioritize mental health, stress relief, and self-care just as much as physical appearance and performance, leading to interest in activities like stretching and mindfulness.
- **Variety and Choice** - Users enjoy trying different types of workouts, with increasing interest in strength training and high-energy activities.
- **In-Person Experiences** - Users still value in-person experiences, special events, and vibrant studio environments, such as classes that combine music and social interaction.
- **Personal Space** - Users appreciate a less crowded gym with a more comfortable atmosphere, including adequate spacing between equipment and areas for socializing.

Modern fitness generations will research your fitness studio before they enroll, from Google reviews and online presence to community vibe and gym layout. They value openness and authenticity so showcase your facilities and classes online. Build a strong online brand and use Google reviews to create trust with your clients, as modern fitness users seek experience rather than just a workout place. Group fitness classes, community challenges, and club events will spark the sense of "*camaraderie*."

Gym design also plays an important role in attracting younger generations. Nowadays, the goal is to create a beautiful and functional environment to set you apart. Modern gym users value personal space and a relaxed atmosphere.

Since today most gym members also train at home or online, consider offering online classes, a workout video library, or wellness guidance. Keep in mind that social gatherings like themed fitness events, workshops, or social clubs can trigger members to bond over shared interests.

The recent IHRSA Foundation and ABC Fitness Solutions research study "The Next Fitness Consumer" examined the motivations and behaviors of fitness consumers. Results showed that 57% of modern fitness fans name social connection as the number one reason when joining the fitness space.

Figure 5-1 displays how community plays a crucial role in fitness motivation, by different generations.

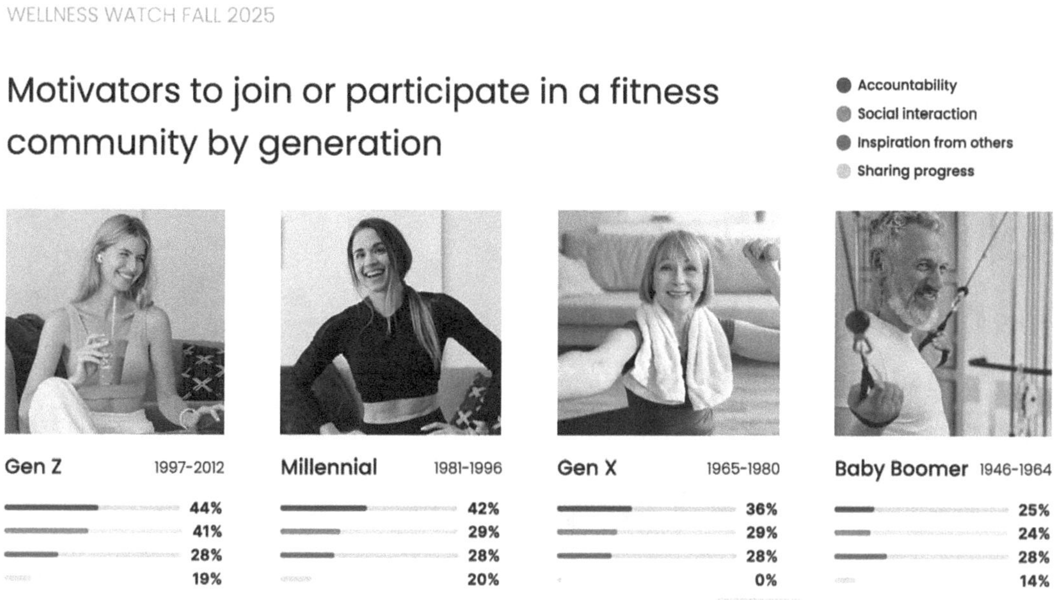

Figure 5-1. *ABC Fitness. How community is redefining fitness, Fitness Wellness Watch Report, Fall 2025*

Younger audiences feel diversity and technology will lead the way in the fitness industry, while older generations think smaller group classes will become more popular, but all ages see **fitness becoming more about holistic wellness**.

The Les Mills report is the biggest study into younger fitness consumers, showing that even though younger generations (*Gen Z*) spend more time on their phones, they are also more diverse, socially conscious, and health focused than any previous generations. They work out for overall wellness and to be part of a community and in return expect flexible fitness solutions to match their lifestyle. Younger fitness users are drawn to the supportive environment of a gym or a studio; they identify the **energy of the community, quick results,** and **active coach guidance** as the key factors that attract them to the gym. With community as the primary motivator, modern fitness fans like authentic content showcasing interaction and connection through members' stories on their fitness journey. Figure 5-2 illustrates the concept of omnifitness as presented in industry reports by Les Mills.

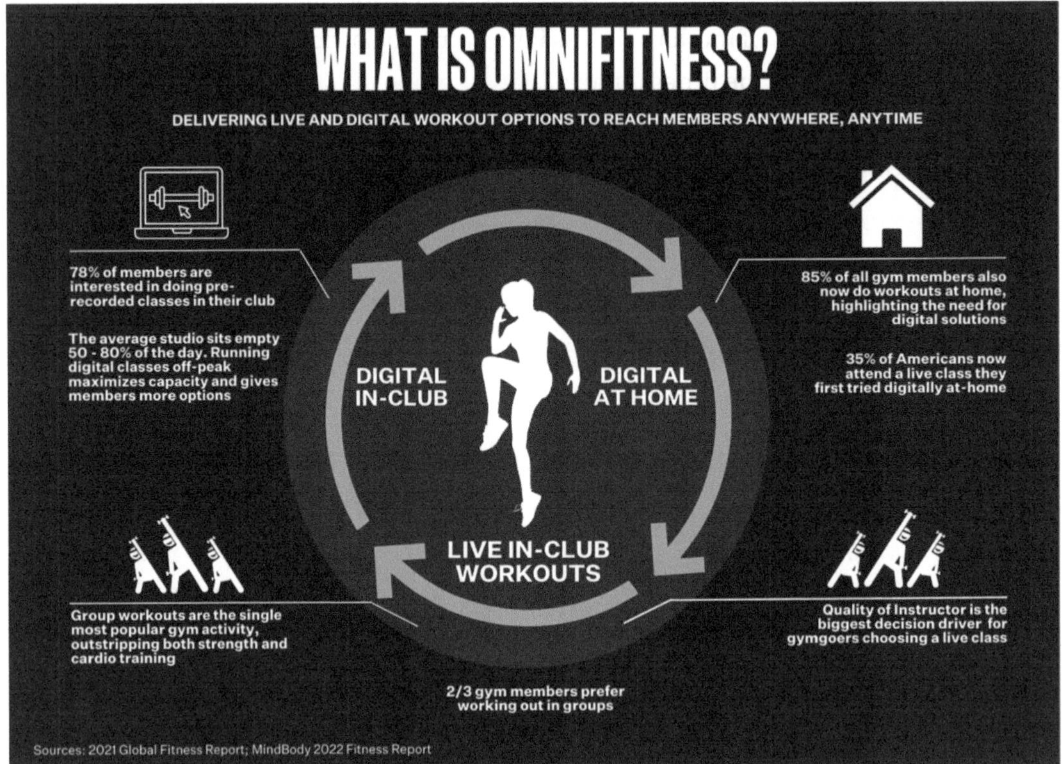

Figure 5-2. *What is Omnifitness. Source: Les Mills, Infographic. Source: Global Fitness Report 2021, MindBody 2022 Fitness Report. Available at:* `https://www.lesmills.com/articles/infographic-what-is-omnifitness`

5.2 Tech Trends for Fitness Lovers

A study by the American College of Sports Medicine (ACSM) found that wearable technology is among the top fitness trends for 2026, with fitness professionals reporting growing interest in personalized and technology-driven workouts.

With wearables leading the way, there are other major tech trends, as follows, that users can benefit from.

Wearable Technology and Fitness Trackers

One of the top fitness trends is wearable technology. Fitness trackers and smartwatches, such as Apple Watch or Fitbit and Garmin devices, became part of everyday routines for many fitness enthusiasts. These devices monitor a wide range of metrics (e.g., *heart rate, steps, sleep quality,* and even *stress levels*) over a certain period. You can set your goals no matter if you want to walk 1000 steps a day or complete a set of workouts in a week. Additionally, real-time data help you stay active and consistent in your workout.

Wearables will provide you with the personalization and real-time feedback that will help you better understand your body and adapt your fitness exercises accordingly.

Fitness Mobile/Web Apps

Fitness apps allow you to access guided classes without having to pay a gym membership.

These apps support your goals with personalized workout plans based on your individual preferences (e.g., *strength training, cardio*), while AI-driven coaches provide guidance with audio/video cues for a quality training at home or on the go. Some apps can help you track nutrition, providing diet details to help you stay consistent in your workout.

The fitness app examples include MyFitnessPal, Strava, Nike Training Club, or Peloton offering personalized workout plans and/or virtual classes. With many diverse fitness apps available, you can tailor your experience to fit your needs and resources, no matter if you want to work out at home or in a gym setting. As shown in Figure 5-3, fitness tracking applications typically feature a structured user interface that guides users from onboarding screens to personalized profiles and training programs.

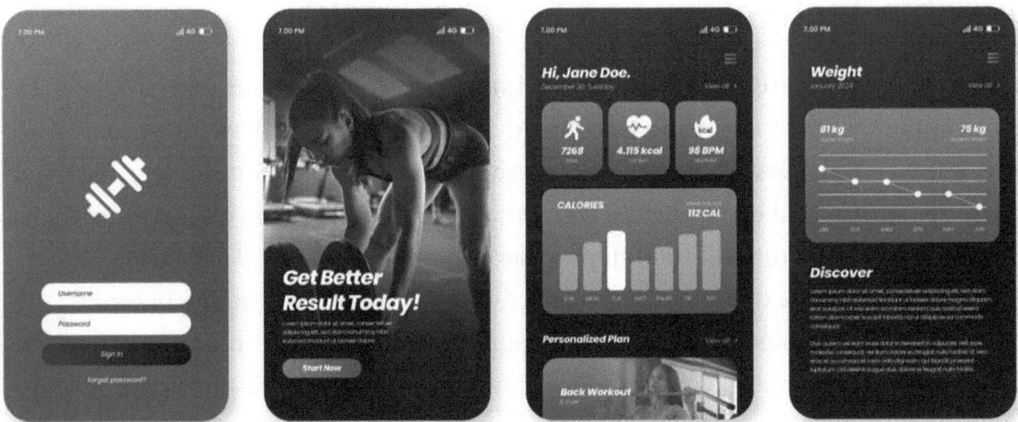

Figure 5-3. *User interface design of a fitness tracking application by Freepik. Available at:* `https://www.freepik.com`

Virtual Workouts and On-Demand Classes

Virtual and on-demand fitness classes gain popularity in response to the pandemic period. Platforms like Peloton, Beachbody On Demand, and YouTube fitness channels offer users to join group workouts from their homes.

These platforms provide you with convenience to participate in workouts anytime and anywhere, with a wide range of workout types that serve all fitness levels and preferences. Live classes with real engagement from trainers and other users provide a sense of community, even if you train remotely.

Flexible scheduling and social engagement make it easier to stick to your fitness goals and meet others who share similar goals.

Smart Home Fitness Equipment

With smart fitness machines like the Peloton bike and Tonal, you can bring *"the gym into your home"* and train with the help of guided workouts.

These machines provide live or on-demand classes guided by professionals and integrate with fitness apps and wearables – as your fitness levels improve, these smart devices adjust the workout pace and make your exercises more challenging.

Smart home fitness equipment helps people maintain their workout routines without leaving home.

Virtual Reality (VR) and Augmented Reality (AR) Fitness

Companies like Supernatural and FitXR offer immersive fitness experiences where training meets gamification, making workouts fun and engaging.

VR and AR fitness enables you to "*travel*" to panoramic locations while training (*boxing, HIIT, etc.*). These platforms make fitness engaging and enjoyable as you earn points or compete with other members in virtual space.

This game-like approach helps you join workouts in an entirely new way, acting as an effective way to achieve your fitness goals. As shown in Figure 5-4, virtual reality (VR)-based fitness training enables users to engage in immersive exercise experiences, such as cycling in simulated environments.

Figure 5-4. *Image of a user participating in VR-based fitness training. Image by Freepik. Available at:* `https://www.freepik.com`

5.3 Software Fitness Solutions (*Mobile Apps, Online Training, etc.*)

Fitness software solutions are digital tools that guide your training entirely via applications (mobile/web), where you do not need any physical devices to train.

Check out below the list of the **core categories of fitness software**, all accessible via a phone or a computer.

Fitness Mobile and Web Apps

The broad adoption of fitness applications across diverse populations started during the pandemic period with downloads increasing by 46%, resulting in over 84% of smartphone users having at least one fitness app installed.

Fitness apps offer a variety of tailored exercise routines (*strength, cardio, etc.*), while integrated tracking features monitor your fitness progress. Some apps offer live/on-demand classes or social features so you can share achievements or join challenges, but most apps integrate with wearables (e.g., *smartwatches, fitness bands*) enabling you to closely monitor your activity levels. (Check the section "Hybrid Fitness Solutions (*Wearables and Connected Devices*).")

Fitness apps deliver guided workouts to your phone or a device (video/audio) and usually offer affordable subscription models, making quality fitness workouts accessible for a wider audience.

Some examples of fitness apps include **Freeletics** (*bodyweight, HIIT*), **Nike Training Club** (*varied workouts: mobility, strength, cardio*), and **Aaptiv** (*audio-led workouts for running, strength, mobility*) or, if you want more targeted workout, **StretchIt** (*progressive flexibility goals*), **The Pole PT** (*structured, targeted programs for shoulder mobility, core strength, back flexibility, etc.*), and more. As shown in Figure 5-5, the Pole PT fitness application provides a structured cross-training interface that categorizes workouts into areas such as shoulders, core, strength, mobility, and flexibility.

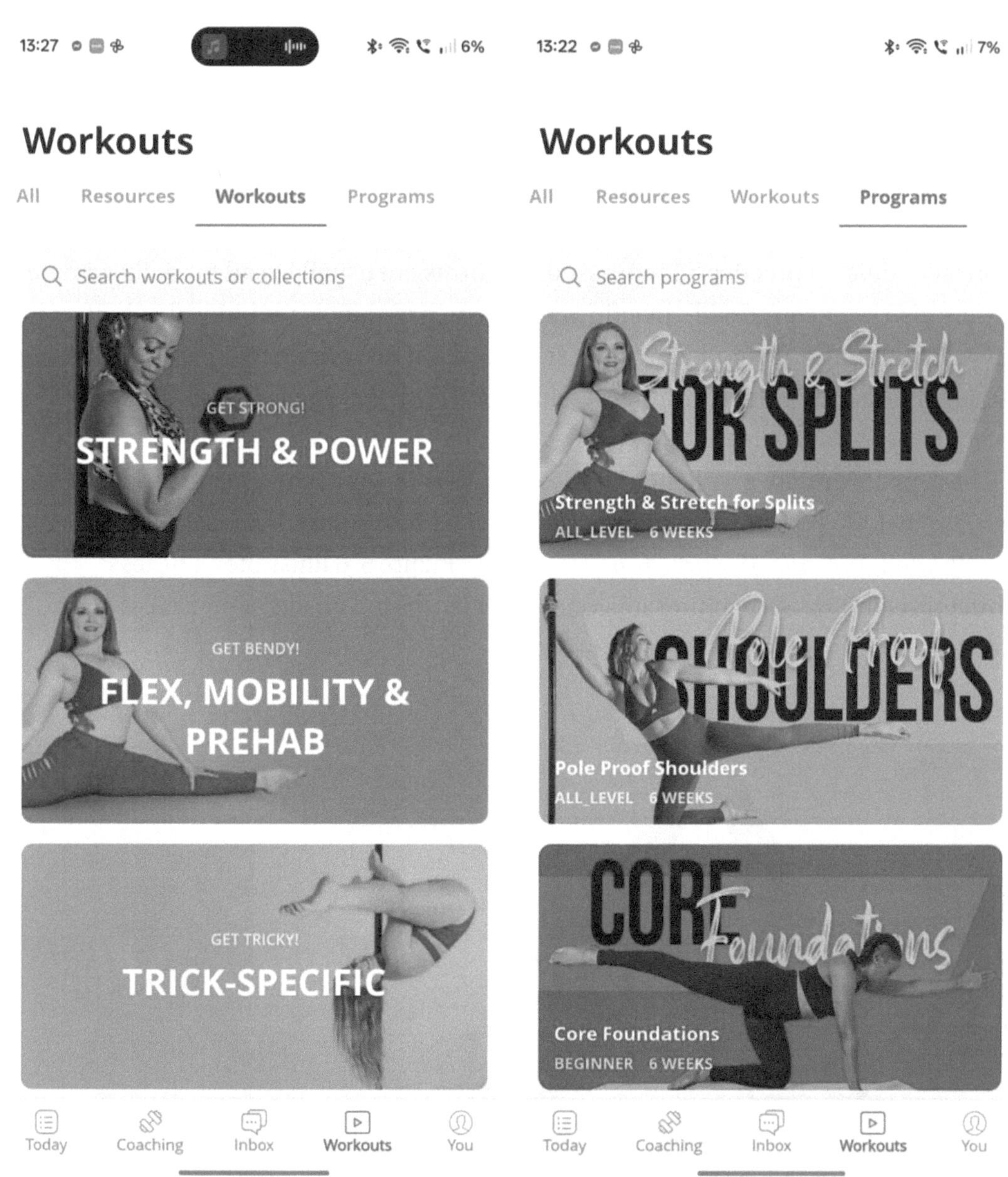

Figure 5-5. *Interface of The Pole PT fitness app showing the cross-training workout with categories such as shoulders, core, strength, mobility, flexibility, etc. Image courtesy of The Pole PT. Used with permission*

Video-Based (On-Demand) Fitness Platforms

Video-based fitness platforms offer **pre-recorded workouts** you can access via a phone, tablet, or computer, thereby increasing accessibility to a broader demographic.

Watching the way movements are executed will help you better understand technique, plus you can watch these videos at your own convenience and easily adapt it to your schedule. In practice, video-based platforms are usually used for daily workouts. They are also popular for skill-specific practice, such as dance, mobility, flexibility, or bodyweight training, where seeing precise movement performance is essential. You can choose from various guided training sessions (*HIIT, cardio, yoga, etc.*) so you do not have to plan the workout yourself.

These platforms are excellent as they can always fit your schedule. Popular examples include *Beachbody on Demand (21-Day Fix, Insanity, etc.), Daily Burn, Peloton App, and YouTube fitness channels.* Figure 5-6 illustrates a fitness instructor recording a stretching session for a video-based on-demand fitness class, reflecting the growth of digital fitness solutions.

Figure 5-6. *Fitness instructor recording a stretching session for a video-based on-demand fitness class by Freepik. Available at:* `https://www.freepik.com`

Live-Stream Classes/Virtual Group Workouts

Live-stream classes and virtual group workouts imitate the energy and structure of a live class through a screen. When you train at a certain time with others, you get a sense of shared effort that reflects a real gym environment.

One of the key advantages of live classes is **instant feedback** you receive through real-time cues, questions, or interaction with the instructor (*chat/video*). Seeing others training with you can boost engagement and consistency, even when everyone is physically apart.

Examples include Obé Fitness (*daily live classes + on-demand, various styles: HIIT, yoga, dance, etc.*), NEOU Fitness (*mix of live + streamed workout classes from boutique studio instructors*), Daily Burn (*live scheduled workout, broad library of on-demand for different fitness goals*), and Barry's (*previously Berry's Bootcamp, instructor-led live classes, known for HIIT, etc.*).

Personal and Online Coaching

Personal and online coaching is personalized **training delivered via digital platforms**, combining **human guidance and software benefits**.

Instead of generic programs, you receive customized workout plans tailored to your goals while a coach provides guidance as you progress. Online coaching removes location barriers, allowing you to train with fitness experts worldwide and offering more flexibility than traditional training.

Some popular examples include platforms like Future (*personalized workouts and one-on-one coaching*), TrainHeroic (*coach-led programs*), TrueCoach (*trainer-centric platform for customized plans*), Trainerize (*connects coaches and clients with tailored workouts*), and more.

Interactive and Smart Training Software

Interactive training software refers to **digital fitness platforms that respond to user input in real time**, usually using AI or similar technology. These programs **personalize workouts on the go** based on your performance, progress, and goals.

For example, a smart training software can adapt the intensity of exercises if you complete them easily or suggest modifications if you struggle with certain movements. The main benefits are **adaptive programs and targeted progression**, while gamified experience keeps your motivation high.

This type of training software **acts like a personal coach in digital form**, adjusting to your needs in real time while providing guidance.

Examples include Freeletics AI Coach (*AI-driven platform creating adaptive plans tailored to your feedback and results*), Fitbod (*personalized training plans, adapting future sessions per your metrics*), and Future (*AI + human coaching via app*).

Augmented and Virtual Reality Fitness Software

Unlike standard apps, these platforms use **AR (augmented reality)** or **VR (virtual reality)** to guide and motivate you in real time. For example, an AR workout app can project visual cues on your environment to show correct movements, while a VR platform can place you in a fully virtual fitness studio, where training feels like part of an adventure. In simple words, immersive fitness software uses *virtual worlds, visual feedback, and gamified elements* to make workouts feel more like fun, rather than just exercise.

The main benefits are **engagement and feedback** - the AR/VR platforms can track progress, provide adaptive challenges, and make repetitive movements feel fun. This is especially popular for bodyweight or functional exercises and coordination-based workouts (e.g., *dance*).

Examples include Les Mills XR Dance (*immersive, AR-style dance experience*), Tempo Fit App (*interactive + semi-immersive AI-guided training*), FitXR (*VR platform offering boxing, dance, and HIIT workouts*), Supernatural (*VR workouts set in virtual locations with guided movement and music*), and more.

Educational and Skill-Learning Fitness Software

Skill-learning platforms focus on teaching, refining, and **mastering techniques**, while educational fitness similarly focuses on **teaching skills and techniques** rather than just guiding a workout. Together, these platforms often include **step-by-step tutorials or courses** for improving form, understanding movement mechanics, or learning new disciplines (e.g., *dance, calisthenics, pole dance*). Skill-learning programs usually include quizzes, structured lesson plans, or progression markers to measure mastery and results.

Popular examples include Udemy/Skillshare fitness courses, MoveU Academy, pole or dance online academies (subscription platforms), and skill-focused YouTube tutorials.

Community-Driven Fitness Platforms

These types of fitness platforms **prioritize social connection** and group motivation, rather than just guiding workouts.

They allow you to connect with others who have similar goals, participate in challenges, share progress, and celebrate achievements together. The focus is on **community support**, which can increase motivation, especially for users who enjoy a social or competitive atmosphere.

These platforms can link to fitness wearables, but also include

- Group challenges or leaderboards to compete or collaborate with others
- Forums or chats for sharing progress and discussing topics
- Reminders and streaks to help you stay consistent

Popular examples include Strava (tracks running, cycling, and other workouts with GPS tracking and social features), MyFitnessPal Community (forums where users share tips), Discord fitness communities, Facebook groups for fitness programs, and more.

Technology not only made fitness more accessible to a wider population but also enabled individuals to take lead in their health journeys. No matter if you are just a beginner or an experienced athlete, the right technology tools will provide you with personalized data insights and motivation to drive better results.

As technology continues to evolve, the future of fitness will become more innovative and more dynamic.

5.4 Hybrid Fitness Solutions (*Wearables and Connected Devices*)

Hybrid fitness solutions are technology solutions that use connected devices to obtain real-time data from the user body and workouts. These tools are the foundation of hybrid fitness systems, where physical activity is connected to software platforms and wearable devices.

Wearable Technology

Wearable technology or "**wearables**" are types of electronic devices that you can wear as an accessory, embedded in clothes or on the body and most recently even tattooed on the skin. These devices are powered by microprocessors and can send and receive data via the Internet. The wide adoption has ranked wearable technology at the top of the Internet of Things (IoT) trends.

Let's take a quick look at how wearable technology evolved over time and shaped the way we train today:

- The concept of wearable tech started with basic pedometers and heart rate monitors back in the **1960s–1980s**. At the time, athletes used hefty devices to track steps and heartbeat when training.
- During the **1990s**, devices became smaller and more portable. Digital heart rate monitors and simple fitness trackers became popular among runners and fitness enthusiasts.
- As of **2009**, the Smart Era begins - with the launch of *Fitbit* (2009), *Apple Watch* (2015), and similar fitness trackers, wearables made personal health monitoring a standard.
- From **2010 onward**, wearables evolved into hybrid fitness solutions like connected gym equipment, AI-driven coaching, smart apparel, and integration with fitness apps.

Today, wearables support real-time performance analysis, virtual coaching, and community challenges, unifying digital and live fitness experience.

Figure 5-7 highlights the key milestones in the evolution of wearables.

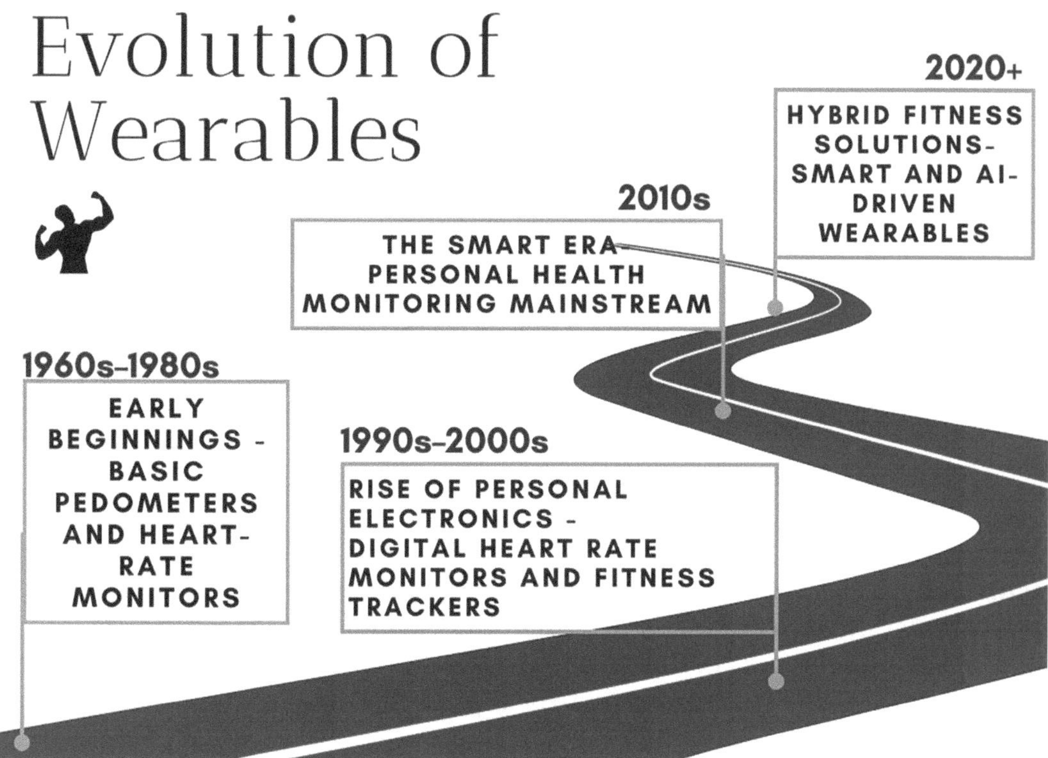

Figure 5-7. *Evolution of wearable technology, highlighting key milestones in the development of wearable devices across different years. Source: Created by the author*

How Wearable Technology Works

Modern wearable technology includes a variety of devices, like *smartwatches, fitness trackers, VR headsets, smart jewelry, Bluetooth headsets, and web-enabled glasses.*

Wearables operate using **microprocessors, batteries, and Internet connectivity**, allowing the collected data to be aligned with other electronics (e.g., *mobile phones, pads, laptops*). Wearables have built-in sensors that track bodily movements and provide biometric data, yet they operate differently based on their category (e.g., *health, fitness, entertainment*). For example, smartwatches and fitness bands are worn on the wrist to monitor physical activity and vital signs daily. Although most wearables are attached to the body, some can operate without skin contact by using smart sensors and accelerometers to track motion, while others use optical sensors to measure heart rate and other biometrics.

The common feature for all wearables is that they **monitor data in real time** as shown in Figure 5-8.

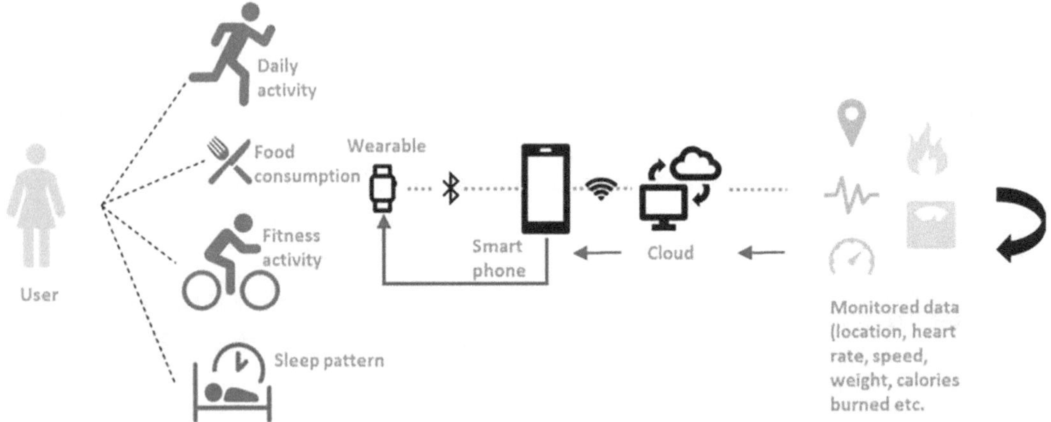

Figure 5-8. *Review on wearable technology sensors used in consumer sport applications. Scientific Figure on ResearchGate. Available at:* `https://www.researchgate.net/figure/Block-diagram-example-of-a-Fitness-wearables-process-This-shows-the-example-block_fig1_332734494`

The focus in the development of wearables has now shifted to more practical applications. Since near-field communication (NFC) or radio-frequency identification (RFID) can now replace keys or passwords, modern wearables include a variety of practical applications like

- **Smart jewelry** (e.g., *smart rings, watches*). Small wearable devices usually work with a smartphone app for display and interaction. Examples include rings like Oura Ring, Gabit, Ultrahuman Ring Air, etc., while smartwatches include examples like Apple, Samsung, Garmin, Polar, and more.
- **Body-mounted sensors** monitor and transmit biological data for healthcare purposes. Includes examples like Polar H10, MyZone, Biostrap, etc.
- **Fitness trackers** (e.g., *wristbands, straps, headbands*) monitor physical activity and vital signs and may connect to an app for data storage, processing, and reporting. Examples include Fitbit, WHOOP, Wahoo TICKR, BioBeat, Activinsights, etc.

- **Smart clothing** with built-in technology monitors health data, interacts with phones, and adjusts material features to match the user's activity. Examples include Hexoskin, Sensoria Fitness, Ambiotex Smart Shirts, etc.
- **Augmented reality (AR) headsets** integrate digital cues into a user's environment, enabling interaction with the real world and virtual reality. Examples include XREAL, Rokid, Viture, etc.
- **VR headsets** completely replace the user environment with digital information and improve the experience. These include Meta Quest, Apple Vision Pro, etc.
- **AI hearing aids** can automatically adapt to provide the best for users' individual hearing needs. Such devices, or "***hearables***," also incorporate features like fitness tracking, audio streaming, and translation. Examples include Phonak (Sonova), Starkey, Oticon, etc.
- **Virtual assistants** can be attached to clothes, for users to control them with voice and gestures. The examples include Bee, Limitless Pendant, and Evie Ring that integrate AI in everyday accessories. The devices can answer questions, find information, and perform tasks similarly to Amazon Alexa and Apple's Siri.

Some of the most influential wearable prototypes, such as mixed-reality devices like Microsoft HoloLens and Google Glass, have helped shape the path of wearable technology, even though some early examples were discontinued after limited adoption. The legacy of these continues to shape the new generation of wearables, including expected Google AI-enabled smart glasses set for launch soon (Warby Parker & Google, 2025).

As devices become smaller and more accurate, wearables will actively **guide training, prevent injuries, and optimize overall well-being**. They will help you improve consistency and form healthy habits through smarter workouts, meaning you can use real data to avoid overtraining and optimize the intensity of exercises.

The new generation of wearables emphasizes wellness intelligence and recovery readiness. Table 5-1 provides a detailed comparison of key features of a few new-generation wearables – *WHOOP 4.0, Oura Ring Gen 3,* and *Amazfit Balance.*

Table 5-1. *Key feature comparison of selected new-generation wearables – WHOOP 4.0, Oura Ring Gen 3, and Amazfit Balance. Source: Created by the author*

NEW GENERATION WEARABLES

FEATURE	WHOOP 4.0	OURA RING GEN.3	AMAZFIT BALANCE
FORM FACTOR	STRAP (NO SCREEN)	RING (NO SCREEN)	SMARTWATCH
CORE FOCUS	RECOVERY, STRAIN, SLEEP	SLEEP, READINESS, WELLNESS	GENERAL HEALTH & FITNESS
DISPLAY	NONE	NONE	FULL AMOLED SCREEN
SUBSCRIPTION	YES ($30/MO)	OPTIONAL ($5.99/MO)	NO
IDEAL USERS	ATHLETES, SPORTS TEAMS	HEALTH & WELLNESS USERS	GENERAL CONSUMERS
BATTERY LIFE	~5 DAYS	~7 DAYS	~10-14 DAYS
LIMITATIONS	EXPENSIVE SUBSCRIPTION, NO DISPLAY	LIMITED WORKOUT TRACKING	LESS ELITE DATA PRECISION

Smart Home-Gym Equipment and Connected Gym Machines

Smart home-gym equipment replaces bulky traditional fitness gear while also offering full workouts. These machines often integrate with apps to automatically track performance, record workouts, and provide personalized recommendations.

With these machines, you can achieve full-body strength or cardio training without going to the gym and stay consistent in training, especially when paired with wearables.

Examples include smart strength systems or AI-driven resistance machines like Tonal, connected treadmills or bikes such as NordicTrack, and interactive workout mirrors that display guided classes and provide real-time feedback. Reformer Pilates and

Rowformer workouts are also popular; Reformer Pilates uses a spring-loaded carriage for strength, flexibility, and balance training, while rowing offers a full-body cardio workout. Rowformer combines both for a hybrid workout targeting strength, flexibility, cardiovascular endurance, core stability, and posture.

Hybrid workouts like Rowformer reflect the growing trend of cross-functional fitness solutions, making home workouts dynamic and engaging.

Smart Textiles (E-Textiles)

Smart apparel, known as **e-textiles**, embeds sensors directly into clothing to continuously monitor health. The sensors enable users to collect data while training, without needing to wear separate devices.

These garments support advanced monitoring useful for performance optimization, injury prevention and rehabilitation. With smart apparel, athletes and fitness enthusiasts can achieve more accurate data, form corrections, and long-term tracking of muscle activation and recovery. They also help detect imbalances or incorrect movement that could lead to injury.

Examples of smart apparel**:**

- **Hexoskin Smart Shirts** – Smart shirts that monitor heart rate, respiration, movement, and activity levels in real time; sync with mobile apps
- **Athos Smart Fitness Apparel** – Garments with integrated EMG (Electromyography) sensors that measure muscle activity, effort, and fatigue; provide real-time performance feedback
- **Sensoria Smart Clothing and Socks** – Smart tops and running socks that collect data on heart rate, foot strikes, and movement technique; can connect to companion apps for trend analysis
- **Nadi X Smart Yoga Pants/Shirts** – Smart yoga apparel with feedback that helps guide alignment and posture during yoga sessions
- **Myant Skiin Smart Shirts** – Biometric shirts that monitor core body temperature, hydration, and ECG; useful for endurance activities and recovery tracking

Smart apparel combines clothing, electronics, and connectivity to create wearable garments that provide real-time feedback, bringing a **data-driven dimension to fitness** that traditional activewear cannot match.

Bonus – Match a Device Type to Your Goals

Table 5-2 presents a mapping between common user fitness goals and corresponding wearable device types and applications.

Table 5-2. *Matching wearable device types with common user fitness goals. Source: Created by the author*

MATCH A DEVICE TYPE TO YOUR GOALS

YOUR GOAL	DEVICE TYPE
GENERAL HEALTH, DAILY ACTIVITY, SLEEP TRACKING, OVERALL WELLNESS	WEARABLE TRACKERS (FITBIT, APPLE WATCH, ETC.) OR A SMART RING (OURA) - MINIMAL GEAR, CONTINUOUS MONITORING
CARDIO, ENDURANCE, HOME WORKOUTS (NO GYM, STABLE ROUTINE)	SMART CARDIO GEAR IF SPACE PERMITS OR INTERACTIVE MACHINES;
STRENGTH TRAINING, MUSCLE BUILDING, COMPACT GYM AT HOME	SMART STRENGTH-TRAINING SYSTEMS (TONAL, MODULAR RESISTANCE GEAR) - ESPECIALLY IF YOU DON'T WANT FREE-WEIGHTS OR HEAVY EQUIPMENT
STRUCTURED GUIDED WORKOUTS / CLASSES AT HOME, POSTURE/FORM FEEDBACK, MOTIVATION	INTERACTIVE MIRRORS / GUIDED SMART-GYM GEAR - MERGES CONVENIENCE + COACH-LIKE GUIDANCE
PERFORMANCE, RECOVERY, ADVANCED HEALTH METRICS, LONG-TERM DATA & FINE-TUNING TRAINING	SMART CLOTHES, PREMIUM WEARABLES, GREAT FOR ATHLETES, REHAB, LONGEVITY, OR SERIOUS TRAINEES
SPACE-LIMITED / APARTMENT LIVING + DESIRE FOR FULL-BODY TRAINING	SMART STRENGTH GEAR (RESISTANCE), MODULAR SYSTEMS, INTERACTIVE MIRRORS - COMPACT COMPARED TO FULL TRADITIONAL GYMS

5.5 List of the Most Popular Fitness Apps and Wearables

The Most Popular Fitness Apps

Here is a **compiled list for fitness users only**, organized by category – it includes fitness, nutrition, and wellness apps.

Fitness and Health Apps/Mobile and Web

Training/Coaching/AI

- **Freeletics** – Bodyweight and HIIT workouts with personalized adaptive training
- **Nike Training Club** – Strength, cardio, mobility, yoga, guided programs
- **Aaptiv** – Audio-led workouts for running, strength, mobility
- **MyFitnessPal** – Exercise tracking, calorie counting, meal logging
- **Fitbod** – Adaptive workouts based on logged performance
- **Future** – Hybrid AI + one-on-one coaching for personalized guidance
- **Shred** – AI-driven workout programs with structured progression
- **Runna** – Running app offering personalized coaching and performance tracking
- **Muscle Booster** – Strength and mobility training with personalized workout plans
- **BetterMe** – Holistic and fitness app with workouts, nutrition, and lifestyle plans
- **Centr (by Chris Hemsworth)** – Training + nutrition + mindfulness
- **Runkeeper** – GPS running tracker owned by ASICS
- **TrainingPeaks** – Training analytics platform used by endurance athletes and coaches

- **The Pole PT** - Cross-training app specialized for science-based training (*mobility, flexibility, strength, etc.*) for pole dancers or athletes
- **StretchIT** - Mobile/web app designed to improve flexibility, mobility, and overall physical wellness via structured video classes
- **Madbarz** - Calisthenics and bodyweight workouts and structured plans
- **Strava** - Training + tracking for running/cycling with coaching and strong social community
- **Adidas Training by Runtastic** - Tracked running and bodyweight sessions with guided workouts
- **JEFIT** - Gym-focused workout planning, logging, and progression tracking
- **Hevy** - Gym workout and weightlifting training tracker with social logging
- **Strong** - Gym workout tracker and strength training planner
- **FitOn** - Fitness app that works like a home gym + personal trainer on your phone with a large library of guided workouts
- **Sweat** - Program-based training app (strength, HIIT, etc.) with structured workout programs
- **8fit** - Fitness app providing workout and meal plans based on your goals
- **Couch to 5K** - Structured beginner running program for building endurance
- **Alpha Progression** - The muscle building app that plans and tracks your workouts
- **Gymaholic** - Personalized guided strength workouts and nutrition logs

- **Hardy** - Gym app for advanced weight training, personalized for your fitness goals
- **Bolt Fitness** - AI-powered fitness app designed for tracking strength, hypertrophy, and conditioning workouts

Meditation/Wellness Apps

- **Headspace** - Guided meditation, sleep, and stress management; beginner to advanced levels
- **Calm** - Mental health app with meditation, sleep stories, and relaxation; more content-driven
- **Balance** - Personalized meditation and sleep plans that adapt over time
- **Insight Timer** - Meditation app with the largest free library of guided meditations, teachers, and talks
- **Breathwrk** - Health app with breathing exercises (*performance, stress, sleep*)
- **Oak** - Simple, guided meditation + breathing sessions

Nutrition Apps

- **Cronometer** - Highly accurate personalized micronutrient tracking
- **Lose It!** - User-friendly calorie tracking and weight loss app
- **MacroFactor** - A science-based diet coach and macro tracker app
- **Yazio** - Calorie counter + nutrition apps + fasting (*popular in Europe*)
- **Noom** - Psychology-based weight loss and habit coaching
- **Lifesum** - App with diet plans and tracking, recipes, and personalized feedback for your goals
- **AteMate** - Photo-based food diary app focused on eating habits, not calories

- **Carbon Diet Coach** - Smart diet coaching app (*popular in bodybuilding*)
- **RP Diet App** - Structured diet based on training goals
- **MyNetDiary** - Digital diet assistant for weight loss with advanced tracking, analytics, and coaching features

Video-Based (On-Demand) Platforms

- **Beachbody on Demand** - Programs like 21-Day Fix, Morning Meltdown 100, Insanity, and P90X
- **Daily Burn** - On-demand workouts with various styles and difficulty levels
- **Peloton App** - On-demand cycling, strength, yoga, running, and meditation workouts
- **YouTube fitness channels** - Free workouts for HIIT, strength, dance, yoga, and mobility
- **Obé Fitness** - Daily live + on-demand classes covering HIIT, yoga, barre, and dance
- **Barry's** - Some on-demand classes available
- **FitOn** - Free video workout app featuring celebrity trainers and a wide exercise library
- **Lumowell** - A range of guided, body-part-focused workout apps with structured routines at home with no equipment

Live-Stream/Virtual Group Workouts

- **Obé Fitness** - Interactive live sessions + on-demand workouts
- **NEOU Fitness** - Live streamed classes from boutique studio instructors

- **Daily Burn** - Scheduled live workouts + on-demand library
- **Barry's** - Live HIIT and bootcamp sessions for users seeking real-time coaching

Personal/Online Coaching (User-Facing)

- **Future** - Personalized one-on-one coaching via the app
- **TrainHeroic** - Coach-led programs users can follow remotely
- **Trainerize** - Personalized programs with progress tracking and direct coach communication
- **TrueCoach** - Personal trainer-led programs with workout tracking and coach feedback

Interactive and Smart Training Software (AI)

- **Freeletics AI Coach** - Adaptive AI plans based on feedback and performance.
- **Fitbod** - Personalized, auto-adjusting workout plans.
- **Future** - AI + human coaching adapts programs to user performance.
- **JuggernautAI** - AI strength training programming platform popular in powerlifting.
- **Zing Coach** - AI-powered personal training with tailored plans, chatbot support, and form feedback.
- **Dr. Muscle** - AI-powered hypertrophy training app with adaptive programming.
- **PUSH** - AI-driven strength training app with tailored plans and adaptive progress suggestions.
- **Gymfitty** - AI-generated strength and cardio workouts.

Augmented and Immersive Fitness Software

- **Les Mills XR Dance** - AR dance workouts with interactive cues
- **Tempo Fit App** - Semi-immersive AI-guided training
- **FitXR** - VR boxing, dance, and HIIT in a virtual environment
- **Supernatural** - VR workouts in virtual locations with guided movement and music
- **Zwift** - Gamified running and cycling in virtual worlds

Educational and Skill-Learning Fitness Software

- **Udemy/Skillshare Fitness Courses** - Learn exercises, technique, form, or disciplines.
- **MoveU Academy** - Focused skill development and movement improvement.
- **Pole/Dance Online Academies** - Learn pole or dance skills via subscription platforms (The Pole PT, DNCR Academy, etc.).
- **Skill-Focused YouTube Tutorials** - Free tutorials for technique and skill building.

Community-Driven Fitness Platforms

- **Strava** - Social GPS tracking for running, cycling, and workouts
- **MyFitnessPal Community** - Forums for sharing tips, challenges, and achievements
- **Discord Fitness Communities** - Groups for accountability and motivation
- **Facebook Fitness Groups** - Social support networks and challenges
- **Freeletics Community** - Online challenges and social engagement
- **Nike Training Club Community** - Leaderboards, challenges, and social sharing

Recovery, Sleep, and Wellness Apps (With or Without Wearable Tech)

- **Rise Science** – AI-driven sleep optimization for better recovery.
- **Headspace/Calm** – Meditation and mindfulness support for mental wellness.
- **Recover Athletics (Strava)** – Prehab and injury prevention guidance.
- **Hyperice** – Recovery tech with compression therapy and massage devices used by professional sports teams.
- **Therabody** – Wellness company that makes Theragun percussive recovery devices for muscle recovery, pain relief, and performance. Additional products include smart goggles, compression boots, and facial skin-care devices.

Holistic and AI Coaching Apps

- **Wellness Coach** – Complete wellness for fitness, sleep, nutrition, and meditation
- **Vi Trainer** – AI voice coach for running and cycling performance
- **Aaptiv Coach** – Audio-guided workouts with AI personalization
- **ArtiFit** – Real-time posture and movement correction using your phone camera

Sports Science, Biomechanics, and Motion Analysis Apps

- **VALD** – Performance analytics systems used by elite sports teams and sports medicine clinics
- **VueMotion** (iOS) – AI-powered athletic performance app that analyzes movements like sprinting, jumping, etc., generating biomechanical reports from video

The Most Popular Wearable Fitness Trackers

Here's a detailed overview of the selected popular brands in the fitness tracker and wearable fitness industry, where each example lists

- *Wearable Device Types*
- *Key Features*
- *Limitations*
- *Best For*

Apple, Inc.

- Devices: Apple Watch Series 11, Apple Watch Ultra 3, Apple Watch SE (3rd gen).
- Apple Watch offers comprehensive fitness tracking with heart rate, ECG, blood oxygen, and temperature sensors, plus iOS and Apple Fitness+ integration.
- Shorter battery life compared to dedicated fitness bands and a higher cost.
- iPhone users who want a smartwatch and a powerful fitness tracker.

Garmin Ltd.

- Devices: Garmin Fenix 8, Garmin Venu X1, Garmin Forerunner 970, Garmin Vivosmart 5, Garmin HRM-Pro chest strap, Garmin HRM-Dual chest strap, Garmin Running Dynamics Pod
- GPS-focused watches with VO_2 max, recovery analytics, long battery life, and detailed training insights for running, cycling, and outdoor sports
- Less polished UI for everyday smartwatch features; may be overkill for casual step tracking
- Experienced athletes, fitness enthusiasts, and multisport trainers

Samsung Electronics Co. Ltd.

- Devices: Samsung Galaxy Watch Ultra, Samsung Galaxy Fit3, Samsung Galaxy Ring.
- Watches and fitness bands with ECG, sleep coaching, body composition, and activity tracking; strong Android integration.
- Battery life varies; integration may be limited for non-Samsung devices; not as sport focused as Garmin.
- Android users who want a smartwatch with fitness and health tracking.

Huawei Technologies Co. Ltd.

- Devices: Huawei Watch Ultimate 2, Huawei Watch GT 6, Huawei Watch GT 5 Series, Huawei Watch Fit 4 Pro, Huawei Watch Fit 3, Huawei Band 10.
- Budget-friendly fitness bands and watches with heart rate, sleep, and activity tracking; solid feature set for price.
- App experience may be limited outside China; not as polished as premium brands.
- Cost-conscious buyers who want decent tracking without premium pricing.

Fitbit, Inc.

- Devices: Fitbit Charge 6, Fitbit Sense 2, Fitbit Versa 4, Fitbit Luxe 2, Fitbit Inspire 3
- Budget-friendly activity and wellness trackers with steps, heart rate, sleep tracking, Google integration, and Fitbit Premium features
- Some reliability issues in certain metrics and iOS integration; more fitness-focused than full smartwatch capabilities
- Users who want a reliable fitness tracker at a reasonable price

Xiaomi Corporation

- Devices: Xiaomi Watch 2, Xiaomi Watch S4, Redmi Watch 5, Redmi Watch 5 Lite, Redmi Watch 5 Active, Xiaomi Smart Band 10, Xiaomi Smart Band 9 Pro
- Steps, heart rate, sleep, and activity modes; very affordable and globally popular
- Less advanced sensors; ecosystem and app may be less robust
- Beginner users or those wanting a budget-friendly tracker

Polar Electro Oy

- Devices: Polar Vantage V3, Polar Vantage M3, Polar Grit X2, Polar Grit X2 Pro, Polar Ignite 3, Polar Pacer, Polar Pacer Pro, Polar Unite, Polar Loop, Polar Verity Sense optical HR sensor, Polar H10 chest strap, Polar H9 chest strap
- Heart rate monitoring and training watches and straps with high sensor accuracy, sport-focused features, and training analytics
- Higher price; may provide more advanced metrics than casual users need
- Trainers, serious athletes, and sports performance users

Gabit

- Devices: Gabit Smart Ring.
- Smart ring and wellness platform integrating fitness, nutrition, and skin/health tracking with a minimal form factor.
- Ring size limits display/UI.
- Users seeking minimal, integrated wellness tracking in a wearable.

Amazfit Active Smartwatch (Zepp Health)

- Devices: Smartwatches Active, Balance, T-Rex, Cheetah, Helio Strap, Helio Ring, AI hearing aid Zepp Clarity
- AMOLED display, GPS, heart rate, SpO_2, sleep, stress, and multiple sport modes; compatible with Android/iOS
- Less precise sensors than premium devices; fewer third-party integrations
- Fitness enthusiasts who want comprehensive tracking in an affordable smartwatch or wearable

Sensoria Inc.

- Devices: Sensoria Smart Socks with Sensoria Core, Sensoria Smart T-shirt with heart rate monitor, Sensoria Smart Sports Bra with heart rate monitor
- Smart garments (*socks and shirts*) with sensors for gait, running form, and biomechanical feedback
- Higher cost, niche market targeting runners and biomechanics-focused users
- Runners and athletes seeking advanced feedback beyond basic features

Ambiotex GmbH

- Devices: ambiotex Smart Shirt with integrated sensors and removable TechUnit
- Smart textile shirts with sensors for ECG, breathing, and movement, for performance monitoring and sometimes medical-grade applications
- Higher cost, niche market, less widespread adoption compared to wristbands
- Performance athletes and users needing detailed data beyond basic activity tracking

Activinsights Ltd.

- Devices: ActivInsights Band, GENEActiv wearable accelerometer
- Wearable activity monitoring platforms for research, clinical studies, and corporate wellness programs
- Primarily used in **clinical research, public health studies, and professional monitoring** rather than consumer fitness markets
- Organizations, research institutions, or corporate wellness programs

Oura Ring

- Devices: Oura Ring 4 (Standard), Oura Ring 4 (Pro/Titanium/Platinum).
- Smart ring for advanced sleep analysis, recovery tracking, and monitoring HRV and temperature. Battery life 4–7 days.
- You need subscription for complete data insights and somewhat limited workout tracking when compared to smart watches.
- Best for users focused on sleep, recovery, and overall wellness tracking rather than active training.

Whoop, Inc.

- Devices: WHOOP 5.0, WHOOP MG.
- Popular wearable for continuous HRV monitoring, strain and recovery assistance, and sleep coaching. No screen involved, app-driven experience.
- Subscription is required; has no integrated GPS or smartwatch features.
- Best for serious athletes and fitness enthusiasts focused on performance optimization and recovery.

Ultrahuman Ring

- Devices: Ultrahuman Ring Pro, Ultrahuman Ring Air
- Smart ring for sleep and metabolic tracking, integrates with CGM metabolic monitor and provides recovery and circadian rhythm insights
- A smaller ecosystem when compared to Oura with limited workout tracking
- Best for metabolic health enthusiasts

Meta and Ray-Ban Smart Glasses

- Devices: Ray-Ban Meta Smart Glasses (e.g., Wayfarer), Ray-Ban Meta Pro, Meta Ray-Ban Display AR glasses, Oakley Meta Vanguard, Oakley Meta HSTN.
- Smart glasses integrate camera and audio, with voice assistant functionality and hands-free content capture.
- They have limited health tracking and certain privacy concerns.
- Best for lifestyle enthusiasts, not traditional fitness tracking.

Google

- Devices: Google Pixel Watch 3, Google Pixel Watch 4.
- Smartwatches with heart rate, sleep, fitness, and Google integration; works with the Android ecosystem.
- Battery life is shorter than dedicated fitness trackers; limited third-party app ecosystem compared to Apple.
- Best for Android users seeking smartwatch functionality integrated with Google services.

Vuzix/RealWear

- Devices: Vuzix M400, Vuzix M4000, Vuzix Z100, Vuzix LX1, Vuzix Blade 2, RealWear Arc 3, RealWear Navigator 520
- AR smart glasses for enterprise and industrial applications; integrate displays, cameras, sensors, and wireless connectivity for hands-free information for logistics, maintenance, and manufacturing
- Niche industrial market; high cost; limited consumer adoption
- Best for enterprise professionals requiring hands-free augmented reality tools

Although we have covered some of the most popular wearable brands, the world of wearables is constantly evolving, making it an exciting space for fitness enthusiasts and athletes. Staying informed will help you choose the right wearable to meet your goals and lifestyle.

Quiz for Fitness Enthusiasts

Find Your Perfect Fitness Tech

Each body moves differently, so not all fitness tech fits everyone the same way - some of us want to track steps, others to improve performance, and some just to make workouts fun. From fitness apps to smartwatches, there is a fitness tech for every goal.

Stop guessing which technology is right for you.

Take this fun quiz and find out which type of fitness technology will help you train smarter. It is super easy - choose your goal, find your result, and discover your perfect fitness companion.

Step 1: What Is Your Main Goal?

- **A. Lose fat**
- **B. Build strength**
- **C. Maintain general health**
- **D. Improve performance (sport-specific)**
- **E. Save time/be more consistent**
- **F. Rehab/mobility/posture**

→ Go to the corresponding branch below.

Step 2: Find Your Goal

A. Lose Fat/Get Active

- **Little time?** → Choose short-guided workout apps.
- **No equipment?** → Choose bodyweight workout apps.
- **Need structure + diet?** → Choose coaching apps.

Best Software Types

Software Type	Why It Fits	Examples
Habit tracking apps, short-guided sessions	Builds consistency; tracks calories, steps, and sleep	*MyFitnessPal, Lifesum, Noom, Fitbit, Garmin*
HIIT/bodyweight workout apps	Fast fat-burning workouts, minimal space	*Freeletics, Nike Training Club, Fitify, Fitbod, Jetfit*
AI coaching apps	Personalized plans	*Freeletics, Fitbod, Aaptiv, Trainiac,*

B. Build Strength

- **No weights?** → Choose progressive bodyweight software.
- **Home gym?** → Choose strength program apps.
- **Gym access?** → Choose structured programs.

Best Software Types

Software Type	Why It Fits	Examples
Strength training program apps	Auto-progression, tracks weights	*Strong, Hevy, Fitbod, PT The Pole*
AI-personalized structured plans	Adjusts load automatically	*FitnessAI, Jefit, Fitbit*
Bodyweight progression apps	For limited equipment	*THENX App, Fitbod (bodyweight mode), 8fit*

C. Maintain Fitness/Stay Active

- **Prefer variety?** → Choose class-based platforms.
- **Low motivation?** → Choose gamified apps.
- **Busy schedule?** → Choose micro-workout software.

Best Software Types

Software Type	Benefits	Examples
Class/workout libraries	Variety: yoga, HIIT, Pilates, mobility	*Alo Wellness, Obe Fitness, Les Mills+, Glo, Garmin*
Gamified fitness	Makes activity fun & motivating	*Zombies Run!, Strava, FitDM, Zwift*
Daily movement/micro-workout apps	Keeps you active without long sessions	*Seven, Streaks Workout, Fiveletics, MoveMore*

D. Improve Performance (Sport, Endurance, Strength Level-Ups)

- **Data-driven?** → Choose analytics/training load apps.
- **Outdoor training?** → Choose GPS-based apps or wearables.

Best Software Types

Software Type	Benefits	Examples
Performance analytics	VO_2 max, pace, load, heart rate zones	*TrainingPeaks, Strava, Strong, Fitbit, Fitbod, Garmin, Polar Flow*
Sport-specific coaching apps	Athlete programs for specific sports	*Stryd (running), Hevy, Runna, The Pole PT, TrainHeroic*
Wearable-linked ecosystems	Deep metrics + recovery	*Garmin Connect, WHOOP, Samsung Health, Oura, Apple Health*

E. Save Time/Increase Consistency

- **Hate choosing workouts?** → Choose auto-generated plans.
- **Prefer someone guiding you?** → Choose coaching apps.
- **Want super-short sessions?** → Choose micro-workouts.

Best Software Types

Software Type	Benefit	Examples
AI workout planners	Auto-generated daily workout	*Fitbod, JuggernautAI, Freeletics, Gymscore*
Online coaching	Human or AI coach	*Future App, Trainwell, Zing Coach, Everfit*
Short-session apps	Efficient and quick	*Seven, FitOn, Lumowell, Streaks Workout*

F. Rehab/Mobility/Posture

- **Injury recovery?** → Choose physio apps.
- **Desk job?** → Choose posture/mobility apps.
- **Tight muscles?** → Choose stretching programs.

Best Software Types

Software Type	Benefit	Examples
Physical therapy apps	Professional rehab guidance	*Kaia Health, PT Helper, PhysiApp, PhysioCare*
Mobility/flexibility apps	Daily stretching	*STRETCHIT, GOWOD, PT The Pole, Pliability*
Posture correction apps	Keeps spine healthy	*Perfect Posture, Upright App, Smart Posture*

Circle your answers, calculate your results, and discover which fitness tech matches your style best.

Select all that apply and see you results; no math needed ☺.

5.6 Key Takeaways

- Modern fitness consumers prioritize flexibility, digital integration, social connection, and opportunities for in-person experiences. At the same time, they seek **variety in fitness offerings**, alongside a **holistic approach to wellness** and respect for **personal space**. While younger audiences believe that **diversity and technology will drive the future of the fitness industry**, older generations expect **smaller group classes** to become more popular. Nevertheless, people across all age groups increasingly view fitness as a part of **holistic wellness.**

- Current technology trends in the fitness industry include **wearable technology, fitness mobile and web applications, virtual workouts, smart home fitness equipment, and virtual reality (VR) and augmented reality (AR) fitness experiences**.
- Software-based fitness solutions include **fitness apps, on-demand video workout platforms, virtual or live-streamed group and personal training, interactive and smart fitness software, AR and VR fitness software, educational and skill-learning fitness platforms, and community-driven fitness platforms**.
- Hybrid fitness solutions combine **physical devices with digital technology**, including **wearable technology (such as fitness trackers, bands, straps, smartwatches, and VR/AR headsets), smart home fitness equipment, connected gym machines, and smart apparel.**

CHAPTER 6

Use of AI in the Fitness Sector

Chapter 6 presents **Artificial Intelligence and its impact on fitness technology** and training. From benefits like personalized workout plans to AI-powered automation of gym tasks, AI is getting increasingly utilized in the modern fitness sector.

6.1 Use of AI in the fitness sector

Although it used to be challenging to find the time to train and stay fit, with the rise of Artificial Intelligence (AI) in the fitness industry, achieving wellness goals has become much easier – whether you just want to stay fit or run your fitness business efficiently.

To understand how much AI has transformed the fitness industry, check the key findings from the report *"AI in the Fitness Industry Statistics,"* which highlights how both fitness users and professionals leverage data-driven approaches.

- 40% increase in user engagement with AI-driven personalization fitness apps.
- 65% of fitness centers are integrating AI-powered tools to personalize client workouts.
- 50% of gym members prefer AI-assisted trainers over traditional trainers.
- 80% of fitness wearables now incorporate AI algorithms to analyze biometric data.
- 62% of personal trainers use AI tools to track client progress and optimize routines.

M. Dakić, *When Fitness Goes Tech*, https://doi.org/10.1007/979-8-8688-2457-9_6

Artificial Intelligence (AI) entered the fitness industry gradually (***late 2000s to early 2010s***), starting with simple customer tasks like answering services, class registration, or statistical business reports.

In the ***early 2010s***, AI appeared through basic algorithms in wearables and fitness apps, analyzing steps, heart rate, and calories to provide summarized yet generic feedback.

As machine learning (ML) advanced, AI adapted to data tracking and personalization. In the **late 2010s toward 2020**, AI brought adaptive training plans, automated progress adjustment, and predictive insights based on user behavior and performance trends. AI-powered fitness apps began tailoring workout plans and intensity to individual bodies, rather than general plans.

In **recent years (2020+)**, AI has evolved into a virtual coach and movement analyst as platforms use various technologies (e.g., *computer vision, biometric information, and generative AI*) to assess form, predict injuries, personalize training/recovery, and support hybrid human-AI coaching models.

Modern AI-driven fitness approaches are usually divided into two categories:

- **Data algorithms** supporting athletes with workout plans, progress tracking, sleep pattern recognitions, etc.
- **Motion analysis** algorithms that improve performance by suggesting technique modifications or coaching diverse movements.

The industry focus has shifted from passive data tracking to active guidance that complements human coaching.

AI in modern fitness supports a holistic approach to health, including not only exercise and nutrition but also sleep and mental well-being. AI has become an important part of people's fitness routines, offering personalized programs that can help them achieve their goals more efficiently. As shown in Figure 6-1, the adoption of artificial intelligence (AI) in the fitness sector has evolved gradually, marked by key milestones in algorithmic intelligence, wearable expansion, and AI personalized coaching.

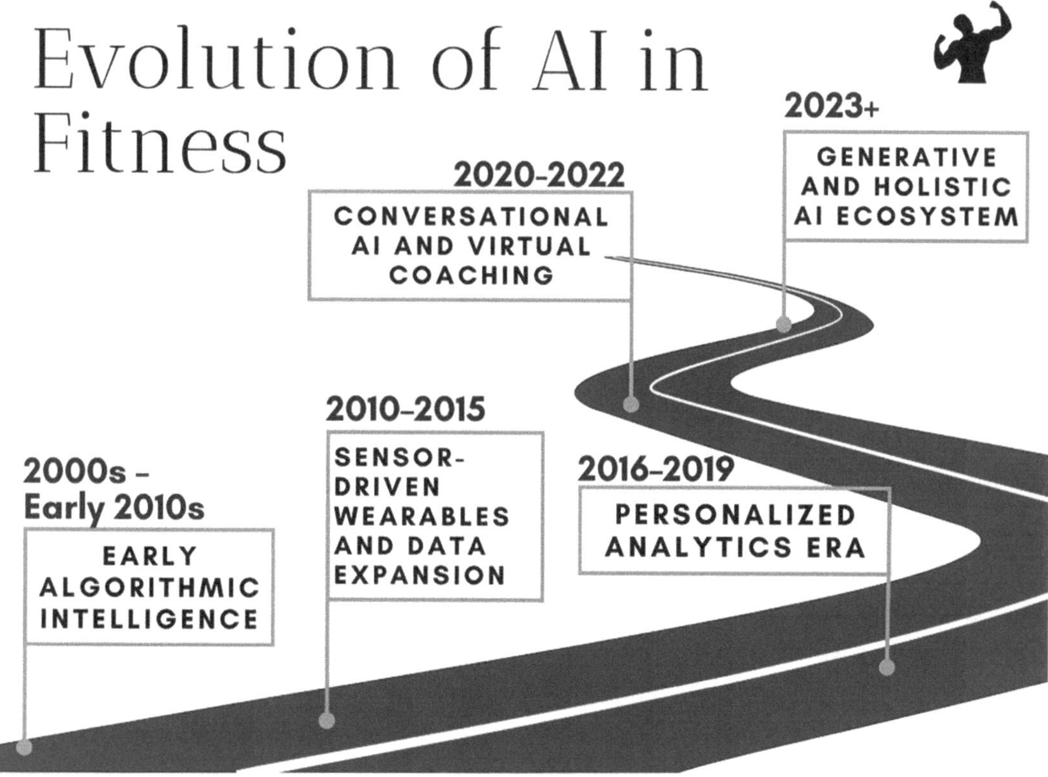

Figure 6-1. *Evolution of AI technology in the fitness sector, highlighting key milestones in its adoption over the years. Source: Created by the author*

Let's explore the key applications of AI that are shaping the fitness industry today.

The most significant applications of AI appear in **personalized training, movement analysis,** and **business optimization**. AI-powered workout apps currently prevail in the digital fitness market (*e.g., strength training, weight loss, guided workouts*) where personalization and flexibility are key features. These apps analyze user data such as training history, performance metrics, and recovery indicators to continuously adapt programs in real time, improving results.

Movement analysis allows AI to assess exercise form using your camera input. For example, platforms like *Tempo* and *Tonal* use AI to track joint angles and movement patterns, providing real-time feedback and reducing injury risk. Another area is **AI-driven body composition** and progress tracking. Apps such as *FitXpress* employ AI-based body scanning to generate accurate 3D body models, enabling users or coaches to maximize health potential.

Modern AI applications cover **nutrition guidance, recovery optimization, wearables integration, and smart studio operations**. One major area is **AI-driven nutrition**, where AI analyzes dietary habits, training load, and body composition data to generate adaptive meal and hydration recommendations. For example, *Lumen* uses AI-based metabolic analysis to determine whether the body is burning fats and adjusts nutrition guidance, accordingly, helping users align dietary strategies with training demands.

Another significant application is **AI-powered wearables and biometric analysis**. Platforms such as *WHOOP* and *Oura Ring* rely on machine learning (ML) to interpret large amounts of physiological data, including heart rate variability, sleep quality, and recovery markers. These systems convert raw data into actionable input, enabling athletes to adapt the workout intensity and reduce the risk of injury.

AI has also been applied in **injury prevention and rehabilitation** through predictive analytics. AI systems analyze training frequency, movement patterns, and historical injury data, to identify early warning signs of overload or imbalance. For instance, *Sword Health* combines AI with remote physiotherapy to deliver personalized rehabilitation programs and to continuously adapt exercises based on user progress.

Beyond training, AI is increasingly used in **fitness business management** to support class scheduling, member retention, and personalized communication. AI can predict attendance trends, recommend optimal class times based on historical demand, and automatically trigger targeted outreach when a member's attendance begins to decline. These AI-powered apps allow fitness studios to improve efficiency without affecting the quality of coaching.

AI is also gaining popularity in **immersive fitness experiences**. VR fitness app FitXR uses motion tracking and real-time performance feedback to deliver boxing, dance, and HIIT classes that reflect workout intensity at home. This shows how AI can improve engagement while focusing on user experience.

The way people define fitness today is not just about workouts - it includes evolving fitness apps, overall well-being, and communities for enthusiasts. The evolution from basic activity tracking to a complete health and wellness system shows how AI has grown to improve every aspect of our fitness routines. From AI chatbots to AI-driven fitness apps, AI became an integral part of the fitness industry. As shown in Figure 6-2, artificial intelligence (AI) is applied across multiple areas of the fitness industry, including adaptive training, performance real-time tracking, injury prevention, and nutrition guidance.

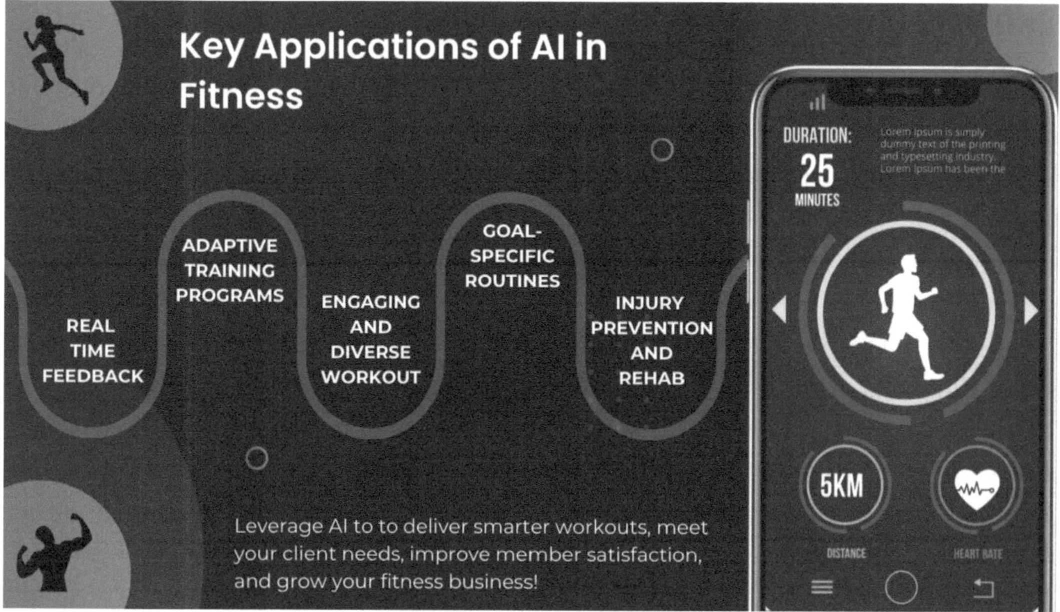

Figure 6-2. *Key applications of AI in the fitness industry. Source: Created by the author*

Challenges and Limitations of AI in Fitness

Although AI-driven systems offer high-level personalization and data analysis, they still come with challenges that users need to keep in mind and developers to address to keep the industry moving forward.

Data Privacy and Security

Since AI fitness apps and wearables collect sensitive personal data (*personal, financial, health metrics, etc.*), it is mandatory for AI tools to ensure data privacy and security. As users become more aware of privacy issues, so do concerns on how this data is stored, shared, and protected.

To address these concerns, AI fitness apps need to use robust encryption techniques to protect data both in transmission and storage. Clear and transparent data privacy policies are essential, informing users what data is collected and how it is used. Regular security audits and compliance with data protection regulations such as GDPR and CCPA help build user trust.

For example, at 3DLOOK, all apps and solutions, including FitXpress, fully comply with GDPR requirements in both the EU and the United States.

Technical Limitations

The power of AI tools in fitness lies in pairing with advanced technology like high-quality sensors, cameras, and stable Internet connectivity - resources that are not always within everyone's reach. These requirements can limit accessibility for users in remote areas or those with older devices, etc.

AI fitness applications are highly dependent on user-provided data. For instance, one major challenge of motion analytics is that you must follow certain guidelines while filming yourself to achieve reliable results. Without these, you may be unable to capture proper video that provides enough input to the AI model.

To overcome these limitations, AI fitness apps can offer features that function in low-bandwidth or offline environments. Downloadable workouts, offline activity tracking, and simplified app versions will help ensure broader access no matter location or device capability.

Accuracy and Reliability

The reliability of AI systems depends on the quality and diversity of the data used. When datasets lack diversity, AI models may fail to account for different body types, ages, fitness levels, or medical conditions, resulting in generalized or misleading advice. Collecting and processing this volume of data takes time and resources. Until sufficient datasets are gathered, AI-enabled fitness applications may struggle to reach their full potential.

Use diverse datasets including a wide range of body types, fitness levels, age, and health conditions. Regular updates and learning models can help refine AI algorithms to provide more relevant and accurate recommendations to all users.

Ethical Transparency and Bias

Bias in training data can lead to possible inadequate recommendations for certain user groups like older adults or people with disabilities while some AI-driven fitness apps may overemphasize specific body metrics, weight goals, or performance benchmarks. This can unintentionally promote unhealthy behaviors, excessive training, or negative body image.

A responsible approach involves implementing guidelines prioritizing overall well-being and healthy habits rather than specific body metrics. Ethical AI design should focus on sustainable health behaviors, inclusivity, and transparency.

When we rely on AI for decision making, one critical problem is that we do not actually know how AI makes its conclusions and recommendations - AI systems must communicate the reasoning behind recommendations clearly to prevent misuse and reduce potential harm.

Regulatory and Compliance Challenges

AI managing health information should be subject to high norms like GDPR in Europe and HIPAA in the United States. As AI fitness apps expand into areas such as nutrition planning, injury prevention, and rehabilitation, they increasingly intersect with healthcare regulations. Apps that provide rehabilitation, or medical-like monitoring may go so far as requiring medical certification. The broader the scope of an AI fitness solution, the greater the regulatory burden related to data handling, consent, and medical compliance.

Developers must carefully navigate privacy laws and healthcare regulations to ensure legal compliance, while maintaining functionality. As shown in Figure 6-3, artificial intelligence (AI) in the fitness industry is associated with several limitations, including data privacy concerns, ethical transparency, high implementation costs, and compliance challenges.

Figure 6-3. *Limitations of AI in the fitness industry. Source: Created by the author*

6.2 AI-Powered Fitness Studio Management

AI-powered fitness studio management is a type of software that uses Artificial Intelligence (AI) and machine learning (ML) systems **to automate, optimize, and personalize how a fitness studio operates**, based on the collected data. These AI systems learn from data like member behavior, attendance patterns, etc., to act automatically and support better business decisions. In short, AI-driven systems predict what will happen next and react accordingly, contrary to traditional software that logs what happened.

AI-driven fitness software is not common today, but it is also no longer *"future tech"* and yet a competitive advantage. Large gym chains and franchises are already using AI for operations like pricing, churn predictions, or marketing automation, while with boutique studios, adoption is growing but selectively. Small studios adopt AI systems less but often use some AI features through smart reminders and automated follow-ups. Fitness studios and gyms that adopt AI early will operate leaner, increase member satisfaction, and scale without overload costs.

AI-powered studio management applies predictive analytics and automation across business operations. For example, AI can **forecast class attendance** using historical data, enabling studios to adapt schedules, class capacity, etc.

Another major function is **member retention and engagement**. AI systems monitor behavioral signs like declining attendance or late cancellations. If any risks are detected, the system automatically sends personalized outreach (e.g., *reminders, tailored offers, targeted incentives*) to re-engage the member. This approach replaces traditional generic messaging with relevant outreach.

AI-driven management also improves **administrative efficiency** as billing tasks, membership renewals, waitlist management, and customer inquiries can be automated through workflows and chatbots. This reduces manual workload and errors and allows your staff to focus on quality coaching and community rather than tedious admin work.

AI also helps with pricing optimization as it analyses packages or classes performing best across different member audiences. Such insights can help you adjust your pricing, introduce new offers, etc., while the system learns overtime which actions lead to higher retention and conversion.

In short, AI-powered fitness studio management does not replace trainers or human interaction. Instead, it acts as a **smart operational assistant** that helps strategic decision-making, scales personalization, and improves efficiency. This way, fitness studios and gyms can deliver a more consistent and member-focused experience while maintaining the human touch that defines fitness communities. As shown in Table 6-1, AI-based gym management software offers enhanced automation and personalization compared to traditional systems.

Table 6-1. *Comparison of traditional and AI-based gym management software (GMS). Source: Created by the author*

TRADITIONAL VS AI GYM MANAGEMENT SOFTWARE: THE DIFFERENCES

OPERATION	TRADITIONAL GMS	AI GMS
DATA USAGE	STORES MEMBER AND OPERATIONAL DATA FOR REFERENCE	ACTIVELY ANALYZES DATA TO DETECT PATTERNS AND TRENDS
SCHEDULING	FIXED SCHEDULES CREATED MANUALLY	ACTIVELY ADJUSTS SCHEDULES BASED ON ATTENDANCE BEHAVIOR
BILLING	RULE-BASED BILLING WITH MANUAL FOLLOW-UPS	PREDICTS LATE PAYMENTS AND AUTOMATES RENEWALS ETC.
MEMBER ENGAGEMENT	GENERIC COMMUNICATION FOR ALL MEMBERS	PERSONALIZES INTERACTIONS BASED ON BEHAVIOR
REPORTING	STATIC REPORTS CREATED AFTER EVENTS OCCUR	REAL-TIME INSIGHTS INDICATING ISSUES BEFORE HAPPENING
SCALABILITY	REQUIRES MANUAL CONFIGURATION AS LOCATIONS GROW	LEARNS FROM DATA AND ADAPTS ACROSS MULTIPLE LOCATIONS
DECISION SUPPORT	DEPENDS ON STAFF INTERPRETATION	CLEAR RECOMMENDATIONS FOR MANAGERS

Let's have a closer look at AI technology and its role in fitness studio management software:

- **Personalized Recommendations** – AI provides insights into the interests and preferences of your members, helps them set their specific goals, and creates personalized workout plans for them.

- **Real-Time Feedback** - With other technologies (e.g., *motion tracking, biometrics*), AI-powered apps help users understand proper exercise technique and how to adapt workout for the highest efficiency.
- **Injury Prevention** - AI systems also detect improper movement and notify users about potential risks.
- **Smart Decision-Making** - AI systems provide relevant recommendations, based on user behavior and historical insights, as well as current trends.
- **Improved Privacy and Security** - AI systems early detect patterns and identify any suspicious activities, to prevent breaches and protect sensitive data.
- **Automation** - AI systems streamline scheduling and member tracking, making gym operations more efficient, reducing human errors.
- **Virtual Chatbots** - AI chatbot are available 24/7 and handle most of the standard questions (e.g., *schedule, classes, memberships*). If a chatbot cannot solve an issue, it will redirect the question to the manager.

Figure 6-4 illustrates the main benefits of AI-powered fitness technologies across different stakeholder groups in the fitness ecosystem.

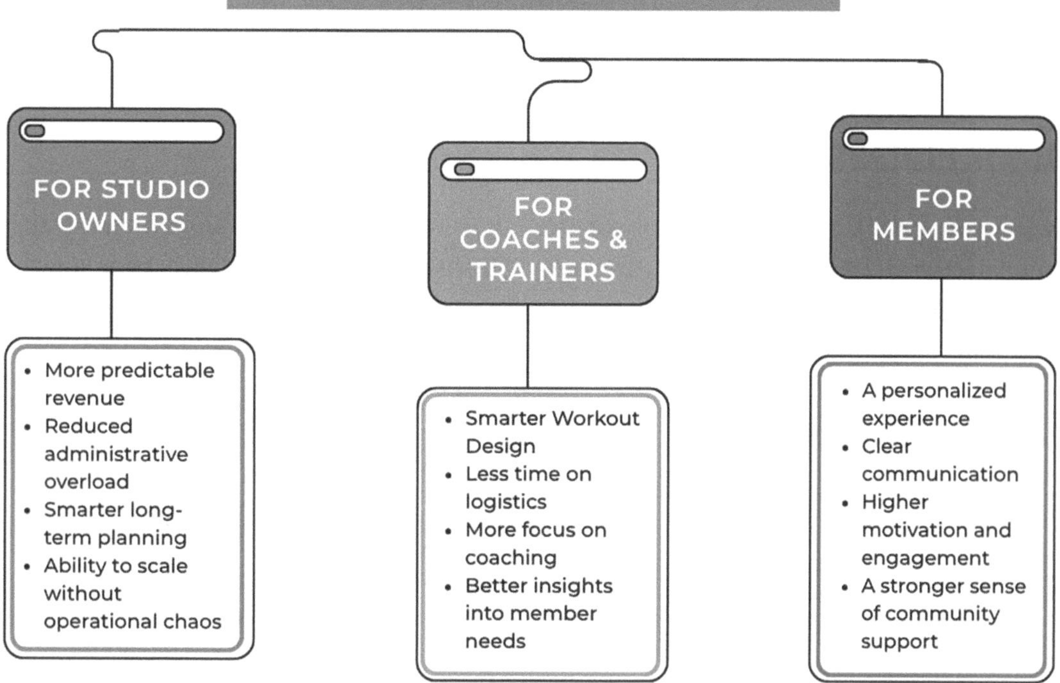

Figure 6-4. *Key benefits of AI-powered fitness for studio owners, coaches, and users. Source: Created by the author*

AI-powered fitness studio management is a **growth booster, not a human replacement**.

Fitness studios that use it operate more smoothly, retain members more effectively, and grow in a sustainable way. Fitness studios that ignore AI as an innovative tool aid will have to work harder for the same results.

6.3 AI Fitness Software Examples

AI fitness software examples below are divided into consumer apps for fitness users and business fitness apps focusing on AI-powered studio management for fitness professionals and owners.

The classification below is divided into

- **AI for fitness users** (consumer apps and devices)
- **AI for fitness professionals** (business and coach software)

AI for Fitness Users

AI software tools serve users to improve training results, adapt the workout intensity to their specific abilities, and optimize recovery. The list contains not only workout apps but also apps for nutrition, posture, etc., and examples of immersive fitness apps and wearables for optimal results.

AI Workout Apps

- **Fitbod** - Workout planner with personalized training that optimizes your recovery
- **JuggernautAI** - Strength training coach, adapts programs for your goals, performance, etc.
- **Caliber** - Hybrid coach combining AI and human coach to adapt progress plans
- **Gymscore** - AI coach analyzing your exercise form with real-time feedback for better technique

Nutrition AI Apps

- **FitGenie** - Personalized AI meal planning based on your specific nutrition needs and goals
- **Noom** - AI platform for personalized weight loss and lifestyle habit building
- **MyFitnessPal (AI features)** - AI coach for nutrition insights and dietary recommendations
- **Lumen** - AI metabolic analysis for nutrition and dietary guidance

- **Foodvisor** – Uses image recognition to analyze meals from photos and provide nutritional recommendations
- **Garmin Connect (AI Nutrition Insights)** – Personalized AI dietary recommendations based on activity and health data

Wearables

- **WHOOP** – AI-personalized recovery and sleep optimization based on your condition and recovery status
- **Apple Watch**, **Garmin**, **Fitbit** – AI health and activity tracking with predictive insights
- **Oura Ring** – Sleep and recovery analytics driven by machine learning
- **Polar** – AI-based wearable for training load and recovery feedback

AI Form Analysis and Motion Tracking

- **Kemtai** – Real-time form correction, reducing risk of injury and improving workout strength
- **Asensei.ai** – AI coach with 3D motion capture and integration of other fitness equipment
- **Tempo** – AI-driven smart gym with motion tracking and repetition analysis
- **CueForm AI** – Form analyzer focused on strength (*squat, bench, deadlift*), with real-time feedback and personalized recommendations
- **Hudl Technique** – Video analysis of user movements to detect technique issues and track progress
- **FormChecker AI** – Video analysis providing real-time feedback and form corrections

Immersive and Interactive Fitness

- **FitXR** - Combination of VR and traditional fitness, including boxing, dance, and HIIT classes
- **Supernatural VR** - Immersive workouts in virtual environments
- **Peloton Guide** - AI-based rep tracking and movement analysis

AI for Fitness Owners

The solutions listed below focus on the business side - *operations, growth, marketing, and scalability* for gyms, fitness clubs and studios, fitness professionals and entrepreneurs, as well as personal trainers.

Studio Management

- **Mindbody (AI-Supported Features)** - AI scheduling, user insights, and marketing automation
- **WellnessLiving** - AI-driven booking, user retention, and marketing tools, as well as analytics
- **Pike13** - Predictive reporting, user behavior insights, and automation of daily operations and workflows
- **Glofox** - AI tools for member engagement and retention
- **Virtuagym** - Studio management with AI-driven coaching and analytics
- **Everfit** - All-in-one AI-powered coaching platform/app streamlining business operations for personal trainers and gym owners

Virtual Coaching (Hybrid)

- **FitBudd** - AI coaching, personalized workouts, and business management (*workout libraries, in-app messaging, progress tracking, etc.*); suitable for personal trainers

- **Trainerize** – AI workout plan creation, habit tracking, and user communication
- **TrueCoach** – Smart coaching workflows and data-driven user insights
- **My PT Hub** – AI-driven performance tracking and workout personalization

Marketing and Growth

- **HubSpot** – AI-powered CRM, personalized marketing automation, and social media management as well as analytics
- **ActiveCampaign** – AI-driven user journeys, marketing, and engagement automation tools
- **Mailchimp (AI Features)** – Predictive insights and personalized marketing campaigns
- **AI Instagram Bio Generators/Caption Tools** – Branding and user acquisition assistance
- **Hootsuite, Later, Buffer** – AI-driven social media scheduling and performance analysis
- **Copy.ai, Jasper** – Content creation for fitness businesses with help of AI

Analytics

- **Google Analytics (GA4)** – AI-driven insights for user behavior and conversions
- **Tableau (AI features)** – Predictive analytics for business performance
- **Power BI** – AI-powered business intelligence and forecasting

Automation and Support

- **AI Chatbots (e.g., ManyChat, Intercom, Tidio)** - Automated client communication, bookings, reminders, and FAQs
- **Zapier/Make.com/N8N (AI-Enhanced Workflows)** - Interlinked automation of booking, CRMs, marketing systems, and various business workflows

AI in fitness is clearly divided into consumer apps that improve personal performance and business apps that optimize operations and growth. For the best result, leverage both - use AI to scale personalization while keeping the human touch that defines successful training and studio atmosphere.

This approach will boost the quality of fitness programs and significantly reduce the risk of injuries by addressing them early. Invest your time in quick research and explore AI tools to find the right solution to cater to your fitness needs, no matter if you are a professional or just a fitness enthusiast.

6.4 Key Takeaways

- AI in modern fitness supports a holistic approach to health including sleep and mental well-being. Key AI applications shaping the fitness industry today include **personalized training, movement analysis**, and **business optimization**. Other important developments include **AI-powered wearables, biometric analysis, injury prevention** and **rehabilitation**, and **immersive fitness** experiences. Beyond training itself, AI is increasingly used in **fitness business management** to improve operational efficiency while maintaining the quality of coaching services.
- Although AI-driven systems offer high-level personalization and data analysis, they still come with challenges such as concerns related to data privacy and security, technical limitations, issues of accuracy and liability, as well as regulatory and ethical transparency considerations.

- AI-powered fitness studio management is a type of software that uses Artificial Intelligence (AI) and machine learning (ML) systems **to automate, optimize, and personalize how a fitness studio operates**, based on the collected data. Key functions of these systems include personalized recommendations, real-time feedback, improved security and privacy protection, automation of operational processes, virtual chatbots for communication, and tools that support injury prevention.
- Key benefits AI-driven systems bring to fitness owners are reduced administrative overload, ability to scale without affecting the training quality, and more predictable revenue while trainers gain more insights into members' needs and progress without wasting time on logistics yet focusing on coaching quality. For fitness users, these AI systems provide more personalized experience with clear communication, improving engagement and fostering a sense of community.
- AI in fitness is divided into consumer apps that improve personal performance and business apps that optimize operations and growth. Invest your time in quick research and explore AI tools to find the right solution to cater to your fitness needs, no matter if you are a professional or just a fitness enthusiast.

APPENDIXES

What Does the Future Hold?

The closing chapter sums up the **predictions and expectations of the digital transformation in the fitness industry**. You will learn more about what the future holds and how the fitness sector can develop further with the help of technology.

The fitness industry is expanding in 2026, driven by accelerated tech innovations, consumer expectations, and holistic health. Digital fitness solutions are no longer optional, as they are now an integral part of how people train, recover, and manage their health. Gyms and fitness studios remain viable by integrating technology and offering diverse services. Since consumers increasingly prioritize convenience and personalized experiences, positioning technology as a central driver will bring you long-term growth.

The global health and fitness club market is projected to reach approximately US$121.58 billion in 2026, growing from an estimated US$111.11 billion in 2025 at a CAGR of 9.4%. This growth is triggered by rising health awareness, increased urbanization, and the popularity of on-demand fitness services. As shown in Figure A-1, the global health and fitness club market is expected to continue growing in 2026, driven by increasing demand for wellness services, digital fitness solutions, and hybrid training models.

M. Dakić, *When Fitness Goes Tech*, https://doi.org/10.1007/979-8-8688-2457-9

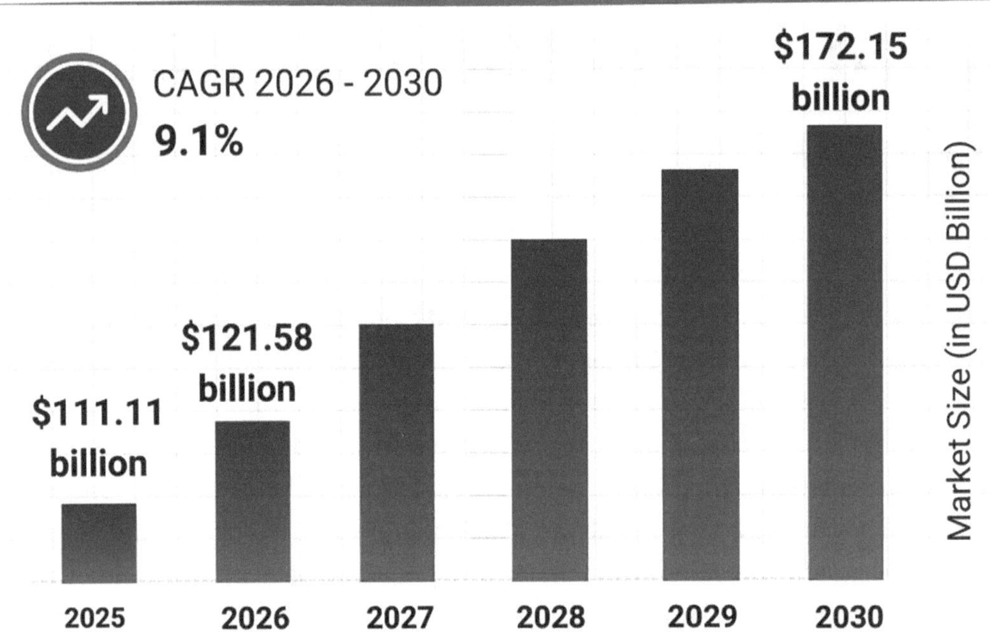

Figure A-1. *Global health and fitness club market trends in 2026, The Business Research Company (2026), Health and Fitness Club Market Report. Available at:* `https://www.thebusinessresearchcompany.com/report/health-and-fitness-club-global-market-report`

The global health and fitness market continues to grow as consumers increasingly prioritize wellness, including mental well-being, recovery, and general health. Due to advanced personalization, real-time feedback, and data-driven coaching, digital platforms outperform traditional fitness models. Besides fitness applications, wearable and sensor technology also triggers increased demand for biometric tracking and performance optimization. Additionally, AI fitness solutions are growing faster than fitness technology in general, indicating AI technology as a future game changer.

Looking ahead, the future of fitness lies in **personalized and holistic experiences**. Meditation, stress management, and mental well-being practices have become integrated into traditional fitness business models, while eco-friendly fitness solutions (e.g., *recycled workout gear*) drive sustainability as key foundation.

Current trends shape the future fitness stage: on-demand services cater to diverse schedules, personalization demand is on the rise, wellness practices are increasingly recognized for their positive effects on mental health, and more. All these trends would not be possible without technology, which plays a critical role in driving these developments, particularly through Artificial Intelligence (AI) and advanced data analytics.

AI technology is transforming fitness by delivering personalized experiences and replacing generic programs with adaptive solutions. As mentioned earlier, platforms like *Fitbod* use machine learning (ML) to create personalized workouts, while AI personal trainers, like *Aaptiv Coach,* adjust workouts in real time based on user performance. Wearable technology further drives personalization with devices like *Oura Ring* that analyzes activity and sleep data for actionable guidance. AI also redefines progress tracking like *FitXpress*, which uses AI to generate 3D body models from photos provided by the user. While the technology behind these solutions may seem complex when explaining, the benefits are simple: faster results, better guidance, and stronger motivation through real-time feedback.

In short, demand for digital fitness will continue to grow as consumers expect integrated wearables, real-time coaching, and personalized workout based on their needs. As a user, you will benefit from smarter tools and more effective training. As an entrepreneur, you can tap into expanding opportunities driven by AI-powered platforms.

With AI-powered fitness advancing faster than general fitness technology and wearables driving advanced health analytics, we are stepping into the future where fitness is more intelligent, responsive, and personalized than ever before.

How Can the Fitness Industry Grow Further with Technology

Let's explore how the fitness sector can develop further with technology and how it could unlock innovative opportunities.

Next-Level Personalization

AI in fitness is all about real-time adaptation and personalization, as it learns user habits, performance, genetics, sleep patterns, and even stress levels to adjust workouts, nutrition recommendations, and recovery plans.

AI combined with genetics can generate ultra personalized programs based on user current condition, injury risk and metabolic efficiency. This approach provides users with training plans designed for optimal performance and injury prevention, which are tailored to user DNA, sleep patterns, and lifestyle habits. AI-powered analysis and progress visualization boost user motivation much more than traditional metrics like weight or BMI.

In the future, systems will be able to anticipate injury risk and optimize training loads, while AI coaches will be increasingly used to personalize training plans along with the user condition.

Fitness As Predictive Healthcare

Modern fitness has shifted from corrective coaching (*"adjust after performance"*) to predictive fitness, where AI helps anticipate injury, burnout, and even health issues before they occur. With AI capabilities, we can send anonymized data to medical systems to monitor public health trends and detect early symptoms, thus turning fitness into an innovative health system.

For example, AI can detect early muscle strain or cardiovascular warnings and automatically adapt workouts to users' abilities or suggest medical check-up. Wearables (*smart rings, clothing, sensors, etc.*) can now also monitor metabolic activity, sleep patterns, hydration, or stress in real time, linking fitness and medical-grade health monitoring. For example, devices like *Whoop* integrate blood test data for more detailed health insights.

This approach can transform gyms and fitness studios into health optimization centers, leading to integration of fitness platforms and preventative healthcare.

Immersive Fitness

Virtual reality (VR) and augmented reality (AR) are slowly entering the fitness industry, making workouts fun and game-like experiences. Users can *"visit"* a digital environment for workout, making them feel more like having fun than just exercising.

For example, while users run, terrain and scenery change dynamically, adapting to user strength and performance. Some market players like *Meta*, now shift investments from VR to AI wearables, indicating how wearable technology currently leads the innovation race.

These types of fully interactive and gamified environments can make workouts as addictive as gaming or entertainment.

Smart Fitness Equipment and Gyms

Smart fitness equipment today encompasses devices that can self-calibrate, provide AI coaching, and adjust automatically without human interference. These IoT systems can track each repetition of users, automatically log workouts, and sync data further without users having to do it manually.

For example, smart weight systems or bikes can adjust load or posture automatically based on users' current biometrics and performance.

With this smart gear, gyms and studios could transform into new age fitness hubs with AI managing attendance, equipment maintenance, and personalized experiences.

Holistic Health Ecosystems

Modern fitness has already started to blend nutrition, mental wellness, recovery, and even genetics into consolidated health profiles. This shows that fitness is more than just exercise - it is a complete holistic acumen that coaches lifestyle. Most of the current fitness tech still focuses on workouts and recovery separately, but the next step is on the rise - a seamless integration of all health data. This type of a unified AI-driven personal health ecosystem would encompass fitness data, medical records, mental wellness, sleep patterns, nutrition, and genetic data.

For example, a platform can combine wearable data, lab results, genetic info, and activity to predict optimal training schedule, nutrition, and recovery plan.

Fitness programs are growing beyond physical workout - recovery practices, sleep patterns, and mental well-being are increasingly integrated into training experience, showing a broader meaning of wellness. This approach allows studios to create genuine holistic health plans for their members.

Eco-Smart Fitness

Fitness infrastructure is predicted to lean into sustainability with energy-efficient equipment, self-powered machines, AI-driven systems, and more. Some also predict that sustainability can even extend to digital carbon tracking for fitness equipment and studio operations.

For example, you can adjust AI-driven lighting systems based on the class type, occupancy, and energy-saving models. Such energy-efficient gear and AI-optimized studio operations could reduce environmental impact.

Future gyms could become eco-smart hubs where AI optimizes energy usage and equipment efficiency in real time.

AI-Driven Social Motivation

Technology can support social motivation, where AI can predict declining user interest and respond with personalized nudges or incentives. Besides simple gamification, social motivation can include community matchmaking, live AI coaching, and habit building.

For example, a system can monitor user engagement and detect if a user is inactive for a certain period - it will automatically send them a custom message or incentive.

With AI coaches, common wearables, and online fitness platforms, you can deliver expert guidance to anyone with a smartphone. Technology makes personalized fitness accessible to a wider audience, including underserved communities and individuals with chronic conditions or disabilities.

For example, AI can support remote rehabilitation programs for people in rural areas or with limited mobility, customizing exercises for their specific abilities and progress.

Some practical developments we already witness are **predictive health** as AI has shifted from reactive to responsive coaching that detect overtraining risk or potential health issues before they show. Mobile/web apps have provided a **connected health environment** with wearables, sleep patterns, nutrition logs, and even medical biomarkers. Fitness platforms have already integrated **social features** (e.g., *leaderboards, shared goals*) to make the user experience more fun, while fitness clubs gradually evolve into **holistic studios** that blend physical workout with recovery tech and overall well-being. AI coaches and smart wearables are making expert guidance accessible to everyone, including the underserved population.

Strategic advantages for fitness businesses are numerous - from personalized experiences for keeping members engaged to AI-driven training and gamified challenges for driving community building. Integrating technology tools and positioning fitness as part of holistic health will expand your reach and make your business stand out in today's competitive fitness market.

Looking ahead, fitness will increasingly function as a form of predictive healthcare, where AI, wearables, and data analytics provide proactive health management. This transformation will create significant opportunities for innovation, sustainability, and meaningful human-centered fitness experiences across both digital platforms and physical studios.

Technology isn't an *add-on* anymore - it has become the **core foundation** of how people train, recover, monitor health, and stay motivated. Consumers now expect real-time data, personalized programs, and seamless integration between devices and platforms. AI, wearables, AR/VR, and data ecosystems are turning fitness from a *routine* into a *smart, adaptive experience* that evolves with the user.

What Does the Future Hold

Wearables are predicted to evolve into health companions (*not just fitness trackers*) while AI is expected to be the key competitive advantage, as platforms that deliver smart insights and predictions will win. Additionally, immersive tech will redefine engagement with real growth in smart personalization. Fitness and healthcare will join forces in preventive wellness, where the industry revenue will continue rising as consumers prioritize wellness. Consumers' interest in fitness apps will remain high while popular apps will shift toward on-demand and personalized experiences.

The next frontier of fitness is not more apps or wearables - it is **predictive, immersive, and hyper-personalized fitness ecosystems** where AI, data, and technology transform **how we train, recover, and maintain health**, while making gyms more efficient, inclusive, and sustainable.

As digital tools become more intelligent, fitness experiences will continue shifting toward adaptive, user-centered environments that support long-term engagement, performance, and overall well-being.

Overall, the future of the fitness industry is shaped by the combination of **technology, personalization, and holistic health**, while creating new opportunities for innovation and sustainable growth across the industry.

The future of fitness lies in creating personalized experiences that serve specific preferences and goals of each consumer. Besides personalization, **holistic approach and the integration of sustainability practices** will also be key trends for the future in the fitness industry.

Key Takeaways

- The fitness industry in 2026 is experiencing growth driven by accelerated technological innovations and rising consumer expectations. Digital fitness solutions are no longer optional, and gyms and fitness studios must integrate technology and offer diversified services to remain competitive and relevant.
- The fitness sector has significant opportunities for further development through innovations such as *hyper-personalization, fitness as predictive healthcare, immersive fitness experiences, smart equipment and studios, holistic health ecosystems, eco-smart fitness,* and *AI-driven motivation.* These trends are reshaping how consumers interact with fitness offerings and how businesses operate.
- The future of fitness lies in personalized and holistic experiences – fitness will increasingly function as a form of predictive healthcare, where AI, wearables, and data analytics provide proactive health management. This will drive opportunities for innovation, sustainability, and human-focused fitness experiences across both digital platforms and physical facilities.
- Technology isn't an add-on – it's become the **core infrastructure** for training, recovery, health monitoring, and motivation. Success in the future fitness industry will depend on creating unique, personalized experiences that align with individual goals and preferences. Besides personalization, **a holistic approach** and the integration **of sustainability practices** will remain the key trends shaping the sector's growth.

APPENDIXES

All You Need in One Place

Appendix A: Gym Management Software

Studio management platforms for fitness entrepreneurs and personal trainers

- **Arketa** – `https://www.arketa.co` – All-in-one fitness and wellness business platform built for studios, gyms, personal trainers, and wellness entrepreneurs
- **ClubReady** – `https://www.clubready.com` – Full GMS used by franchises and boutique clubs
- **Exercise.com** – `https://www.exercise.com` – Custom-branded fitness platform for scheduling, CRM, ecommerce, workout programming, hybrid training, and PT management
- **Everfit** – `https://everfit.io/` – All-in-one platform for small fitness studios and personal trainers with client management, CRM, branded apps, and workout programming
- **Glofox** – `https://www.glofox.com` – Boutique fitness platform with branded apps, schedules, CRM, payments, and automated engagement
- **GymCatch** – `https://www.gymcatch.com` – Simple class/appointment booking, payments, livestream/on-demand support
- **Gymdesk** – `https://www.gymdesk.com` – Clean interface for managing memberships, billing, scheduling, and attendance

M. Dakić, *When Fitness Goes Tech*, https://doi.org/10.1007/979-8-8688-2457-9

- **GymMaster** - https://www.gymmastersoftware.com - Membership, billing, scheduling, attendance, access control, and performance analytics for gyms
- **Hapana** - https://hapana.com - Enterprise fitness platform providing CRM, sales tools, and member engagement
- **Jackrabbit Fitness** - https://www.jackrabbitclass.com/ - Class management and online registration software
- **Mariana Tek** - https://www.marianatek.com - Premium boutique fitness CRM used by franchises and multi-location studios
- **Mindbody** - https://www.mindbodyonline.com - All-in-one GMS with bookings, payments, CRM, staff tools, and discovery in a consumer app
- **Mindbody FLEX/ClassPass Studio Tools** - https://classpass.com - Management and demand generation platform
- **Momence** - https://momence.com - Booking, membership, and course platform for fitness and wellness businesses
- **Momoyoga** - https://www.momoyoga.com - Affordable booking, passes/memberships, waitlists, cancel windows, and client mobile app
- **Pike13** - https://www.pike13.com - Client management, scheduling, and billing for gyms and learning studios
- **PunchPass** - https://www.punchpass.com - Class scheduling, passes/memberships, reminders, and booking embeds for small studios
- **PushPress** - https://www.pushpress.com - GMS and CRM system designed for boutique studios and fitness clubs (CrossFit/HIIT gyms)
- **RhinoFit** - https://www.rhinofit.ca - Affordable gym software with check-in, billing, scheduling, and optional access control
- **Simple Gym** - https://www.simplegym.io - Lightweight billing, attendance, and membership system for small gyms and dojos

- **Teep Software** - https://www.teepsoftware.com/ - Boutique studio and martial arts management with belt tracking and community features
- **TeamUp** - https://www.teamup.com - Flexible scheduling, memberships, passes, and engagement tools for small to mid-sized studios
- **Vagaro** - https://www.vagaro.com - Scheduling, payments, POS, client CRM, marketing, and reporting for salons, spas, and fitness studios
- **Virtuagym** - https://virtuagym.com - Full gym management plus wellness, scheduling, nutrition, and community engagement
- **WellnessLiving** - https://www.wellnessliving.com - Business management platform with scheduling, billing, POS, loyalty, reporting, and central dashboards for multi-location businesses
- **Wellyx** - https://www.wellyx.com - All-in-one management solution for fitness, wellness, salons, and boutique studios
- **WodGuru** - https://wod.guru/ - Class scheduling, recurring billing, kiosk/QR check-in, and member apps for small/medium gyms
- **Wodify** - https://www.wodify.com - Functional fitness management for scheduling, billing, performance tracking, and membership tools
- **Zen Planner** - https://www.zenplanner.com - Specialized platform for CrossFit, martial arts, and skill-based gyms with tracking tools

Personal Trainer and Coaching Software

- **Acuity Scheduling** - https://acuityscheduling.com/ - Online scheduling software to manage bookings, reminders, and client calendars efficiently
- **FitBudd** - https://www.fitbudd.com - Personal training-centric software platform, with a strong focus on *client engagement, branded mobile apps, and training delivery*

- **Just Coach** - `https://www.justcoach.io` - Simple trainer platform for scheduling, workouts, payments, and client data
- **My PT Hub** - `https://www.mypthub.net` - All-in-one trainer platform with exercise creation, tracking, payments, and client logs
- **MyFitnessPal** - `https://www.myfitnesspal.com/` - Nutrition tracking app with diet, exercise, and calorie tracker
- **PT Distinction** - `https://www.ptdistinction.com` - Extensive customization, automation, nutrition planning, and branded coaching portal
- **PT Minder** - `https://www.ptminder.com` - Trainer-centered client management, bookings, payments, progress tracking, and marketing integration
- **Trainerfu** - `https://www.trainerfu.com` - Branded app for trainers with workouts, messaging, and progress tools
- **TrueCoach** - `https://www.truecoach.co` - Personal training platform with custom workouts, client messaging, and progress tracking
- **Total Coaching** - `https://www.totalcoaching.com` - Custom workouts + nutrition, client analytics, and branded experiences
- **Vagaro** - `https://www.vagaro.com/en-gb/pro` - Gym management software for fitness, beauty, and wellness businesses as well as personal trainers
- **Virtuagym** - `https://business.virtuagym.com/` - All-in-one software solution for fitness businesses and PTs for complete member and gym management
- **Workout Labs** - `https://www.workoutlabs.com` - Custom workout creation, progress monitoring, and basic nutrition for trainers
- **WodGuru** - `https://wod.guru/` - Designed for CrossFit and functional training and specialized for high-intensity programs

Appendix B: Fitness Apps and Connected Devices for Users

Fitness apps, wearables, smart home equipment, and AI-powered systems

Wearables + Health Trackers

Smart Watches

- **Amazfit Active Smartwatch** – `https://us.amazfit.com` – Affordable multi-sport smartwatches with GPS and up to ~14-day battery
- **Apple Watch** – `https://www.apple.com/apple-watch` – Smartwatch with activity, heart rate, sleep tracking, and deep Health/Fitness+ integration
- **Coros** – `https://www.coros.com` – High-performance running and outdoor watches popular with elite athletes
- **Fossil Smartwatch** – `https://www.fossil.com` – Stylish smartwatch with basic activity and health tracking
- **Garmin** – `https://www.garmin.com` – GPS multisport watches and trackers with deep training and recovery analytics
- **Garmin Connect** – `https://connect.garmin.com` – A fitness ecosystem for Garmin watches with deep analytics
- **Honor Watch** – `https://www.honor.com/global/wearables/` – Budget-friendly fitness smartwatches
- **Huawei Watch and Band** – `https://consumer.huawei.com` – Value-focused smart devices with fitness metrics and sleep tracking
- **Samsung Galaxy Watch** – `https://www.samsung.com/galaxy-watch` – Android smartwatch with robust fitness and health tracking
- **Suunto** – `https://www.suunto.com` – Premium sports watches for outdoor, endurance, and multisport athletes
- **Polar** – `https://www.polar.com/en/all-watches` – Precision training watches for performance athletes

Fitness Bands

- **Fitbit** – https://www.fitbit.com – Fitness-first wearables with activity, HR, sleep tracking, and wellness insights
- **Honor Band** – https://www.honor.com/global/wearables/ – Budget-friendly entry-level activity fitness bands
- **WHOOP** – https://www.whoop.com – Wearable band focused on recovery, strain, sleep, and performance optimization
- **Xiaomi Mi Band** – https://www.mi.com/global/product-list/bands/band/ – Budget wearable with core fitness metrics
- **Xiaomi Mi Fitness** – https://www.mi.com/global – Fitness and health companion app for Xiaomi bands and watches

Chest Straps and Arm Monitor

- **Biostrap** – https://biostrap.com – Advanced biometric strap tracking HRV, sleep, and recovery. Although consumer products discontinued in 2023, the brand shifted toward enterprise/research wearables.
- **MyZone** – https://www.myzone.org – Heart rate tracking wearable that gamifies workouts (chest strap/armband).
- **Polar H10 + Polar Flow** – https://www.polar.com + https://flow.polar.com – Chest strap for accurate heart rate data for athletes + companion app.
- **Wahoo TICKR** – https://www.wahoofitness.com – Chest strap monitor for HR and cycling integrations.

Smart Rings

- **Circular Ring** - https://circular.xyz - Smart ring tracking sleep, energy, and daily readiness
- **Gabit Ring** - https://www.gabit.com/us/ring - Wellness ring combining fitness tracking with broader health insights
- **Movano Evie Ring** - https://movanohealth.com - Smart ring designed for women's health and cycle tracking
- **Oura Ring** - https://ouraring.com - Finger-worn tracker focused on sleep, readiness, and recovery
- **RingConn Smart Ring** - https://ringconn.com - Smart ring with sleep, HRV, and recovery tracking without subscription
- **Samsung Galaxy Ring** - https://www.samsung.com/us/rings/galaxy-ring/ - Samsung's smart ring focused on sleep, activity, and metabolic insights
- **Ultrahuman Ring Air** - https://www.ultrahuman.com - Recovery, sleep, and metabolic health-tracking ring

Medical and Advanced Health Trackers

- **AIVI Health Patch** - https://www.aivihealth.com - Continuous HRV and stress analytics wearable patch
- **Activinsights** - https://www.activinsights.com - Clinical and research-grade activity monitors; primarily **research-grade accelerometers**
- **BioBeat** - https://www.bio-beat.com - Medical-grade continuous vital sign monitoring patches
- **Levels CGM** - https://levelshealth.com - Continuous glucose monitor system for metabolic health
- **Supersapiens CGM** - https://www.supersapiens.com - Energy management wearable for athletes

Smart Apparel/Smart Fabric

- **Ambiotex Smart Shirt** – Embedded sensor smart shirt capturing ECG, breathing, and movement data. Still exists as a **B2B textile technology provider**, not consumer fitness gear.
- **Athos** (*legacy, discontinued consumer product*) – `https://athos.com` – EMG-powered smart training apparel measuring muscle activation. The company pivoted to enterprise analytics around 2022**.**
- **Hexoskin** – `https://www.hexoskin.com` – Smart shirts with embedded sensors tracking respiration and detailed biometrics. Still active but **mainly research, space, military, and medical studies.**
- **Myant/Skiin** – `https://www.skiin.com` – Smart clothing measuring HR, sleep, body metrics, and posture. Now focused on **health monitoring platforms**, not consumer wearables.
- **Sensoria Fitness** – `https://www.sensoriafitness.com` – Smart socks and clothing analyzing stride, cadence, impact, and running form. Primarily **enterprise, medical, and rehab technology**, not consumer fitness anymore.

Popular Fitness Apps

- **8Fit** – `https://8fit.com` – Personalized fitness and nutrition app
- **Alo Moves** – `https://www.alomoves.com` – Premium subscription platform offering yoga, Pilates, strength, and mobility classes
- **Apple Health** – `https://www.apple.com/ios/health` – Centralized health-tracking app for iPhone users.
- **Apple Fitness+** – `https://www.apple.com/apple-fitness-plus` – Workout platform integrated with Apple Watch metrics
- **Asana Rebel** – `https://www.asanarebel.com` – Yoga-inspired fitness app combining flexibility, bodyweight strength, and wellness routines

- **Echelon Fit** – `https://echelonfit.com` – Connected fitness app delivering live and on-demand classes across multiple equipment types
- **Fitbod** – `https://www.fitbod.me` – Smart strength training app that adapts workouts to personal goals and abilities
- **FitOn** – `https://fitonapp.com` – Free home workout app with guided training videos
- **Freeletics** – `https://www.freeletics.com` – AI-driven bodyweight training, no equipment required
- **Future** – `https://www.future.co` – Remote personal training app pairing users with real coaches for customized programming
- **Google Fit** – `https://fit.google.com` – Android health and activity tracking app connected to Android devices
- **Gymshark** – `https://www.gymshark.com/pages/gymshark-training-app` – Branded fitness app featuring strength and conditioning programs
- **Hevy** – `https://www.hevyapp.com` – Strength and lifting workout app with sets, routines, and analytics
- **iFit** – `https://www.ifit.com` – Interactive training app integrated with connected cardio and strength equipment
- **Jefit** – `https://www.jefit.com` – Popular strength training log and routine planner
- **Les Mills+** – `https://www.lesmillsplus.com` – Streaming workout platform featuring HIIT, strength, and cardio classes from Les Mills programs
- **MyFitnessPal** – `https://www.myfitnesspal.com` – Nutrition and calorie-tracking app with a massive food database
- **Nike Training Club** – `https://www.nike.com/ntc-app` – Free/paid fitness programming with guided workouts

- **Peloton App** – `https://www.onepeloton.com/app` – Subscription fitness app providing live and on-demand cardio, strength, and outdoor workouts
- **The Pole PT** – `https://www.thepolept.com/polept-app` – The cross-training app for pole sport or targeted body part workout
- **Strava** – `https://www.strava.com` – Social fitness platform for running, cycling, and endurance training
- **StretchIT app** – `https://stretchitapp.com/` – Mobility- and flexibility-focused app
- **Strong** – `https://www.strong.app` – Simple and widely used workout tracker for weightlifting
- **Zwift** – `https://www.zwift.com` – Virtual cycling and running platform integrated with smart trainers

AI-Powered Apps + Smart Gym Equipment

- **3DLOOK FitXpress** – `https://3dlook.me` – AI body scanner that produces detailed measurements and tracks physical progress.
- **BetterMe** – `https://betterme.world` – Personalized fitness, nutrition, and mental health AI coaching app.
- **Centr** – `https://centr.com` – Workout and meal planning app with guided mindfulness.
- **CoPilot** – `https://mycopilot.com` – Coaching app combining human trainers with AI-assisted guidance.
- **EGYM** – `https://egym.com` – Connected smart gym machines with adaptive workouts and an integrated app.
- **FORME Life** – `https://formelife.com` – Smart mirror system with interactive strength training and motion sensors.
- **Moov** – Real-time AI coaching wearable for running, HIIT, and boxing. Unfortunately, as of January 2026 the company announced the end of all wearable products.

- **Peloton** – `https://onepeloton.com/app` – Connected ecosystem with bikes, treadmills, and an app with live/on-demand workouts.
- **RENPHO** – `https://renpho.com` – Smart body composition scales connected to a mobile app.
- **SprintFWD** – `https://sprintfwd.com` – Digital training platform supporting brands and gyms.
- **Tonal** – `https://www.tonal.com` – AI-powered smart home gym that adjusts digital weight and provides real-time feedback.
- **Wahoo Fitness** – `https://www.wahoofitness.com` – Smart trainers and cycling hardware with a connected app.
- **Withings Health Mate** – `https://www.withings.com` – Smart scales, watches, and connected health devices with advanced analytics.

Smart Machines and Home Gyms

- **Aviron** – `https://www.avironactive.com` – Gamified rowing machine with competitive workouts
- **CLMBR** – `https://clmbr.com` – Connected vertical trainer with real-time metrics
- **Concept2** – `https://www.concept2.com` – Industry-standard rowing machines with digital performance tracking
- **FightCamp** – `https://joinfightcamp.com` – Punch-tracking sensors and interactive boxing workouts
- **Hydrow** – `https://hydrow.com` – Connected rowing machine with realistic rowing experiences
- **Mirror (Lululemon Studio)** – `https://www.lululemonstudio.com` – Fitness mirror streaming live and on-demand classes
- **Tempo** – `https://tempo.fit` – Smart home gym using 3D sensors for form tracking

- **NordicTrack** - https://www.nordictrack.com - Connected treadmills, bikes, and rowers integrated with iFit
- **Oxefit** - https://www.oxefit.com - AI-driven smart strength training platform used in elite sports facilities
- **Speediance** - https://www.speediance.com - AI-powered cable resistance home gym competing with Tonal
- **Vitruvian** - https://vitruvianform.com - Digital weight training platform using adaptive resistance

Recovery and Stress

- **Apollo Neuro** - https://apolloneuro.com - Wrist or ankle wearable delivering vibration therapy to reduce stress and improve recovery
- **Calm** - https://www.calm.com/ - Offers guided mediations, breathing exercises, and stories aimed to reduce anxiety and relaxation
- **Embr Wave 2** - https://embrlabs.com - Thermoregulation wearable for comfort, stress, and sleep management
- **Headspace** - https://www.headspace.com/ - Guided meditations for immediate stress relief and sleep exercises
- **Healy** - https://www.healy.shop - Biofeedback wellness wearable with microcurrent therapy
- **Hyperice** - https://hyperice.com - Connected recovery technology including compression systems and massage devices
- **Kubios HRV** - https://www.kubios.com/ - Professional app focused on analyzing heart rate for daily recovery monitoring
- **Mindshift CBT** - https://mindshiftcbt.com/ - Uses cognitive behavioral therapy (CBT) strategies to help users manage stress and anxiety
- **Muse Headband** - https://choosemuse.com - EEG meditation headband tracking brain activity

- **ONVY** - `https://www.onvy.health/ai-health-coach` - AI health coach for nutrition, sleep, fitness, and better recovery
- **Therabody Theragun** - `https://www.therabody.com` - Percussive recovery device integrated with guided recovery programs
- **Wellhero** - `https://wellhero.co/` - Sleep, stress, and HRV tracker for iPhone and Apple Watch

Posture/Form and Motion Tracking

- **Asensei.ai** - `https://www.asensei.ai/` - AI coach with 3D motion capture and integration of other fitness equipment.
- **CheckMotion** - `https://checkmotion.app/` - AI-powered motion tracking app for performance and form analysis with biomechanical insights and trajectory visualization.
- **CueForm AI** - `https://cueform.ai/` - Form analyzer focused on strength (*squat, bench, deadlift*), with real-time feedback and personalized recommendations.
- **Darma Smart Cushion** - `https://dar.ma` - Smart sensor cushion for posture tracking (office use). Commercial activity appears extremely limited.
- **FormChecker AI** - `https://www.formchecker.ai/` - Video analysis providing real-time feedback and form corrections.
- **Hudl Technique** - `https://www.hudl.com/en_gb/products/hudl` - Video analysis of user movements to detect technique issues and track progress.
- **Kaia Health** - `https://kaiahealth.com/` - An app that uses a front-facing camera to analyze movement and posture in real time and provide corrective feedback.
- **Kemtai** - `https://kemtai.com/` - Digital motion analysis platform, reducing risk of injury and improving workout strength.

- **Kinetisense** - `https://kinetisense.com` - Wearable motion analysis sensors used by therapists and trainers.
- **KinesteX AI** (emerging tech) - `https://www.kinestex.com/` - Platform offering *AI motion intelligence* that can power posture and movement tracking experiences (often white-label, not a standalone consumer app).
- **Tempo** - `https://tempo.fit/` - AI-driven smart gym with motion tracking and repetition analysis.
- **Upright Go** - `https://www.uprightpose.com` - Posture trainer wearable placed on the back.

Bibliography

Allem, J. P. (2024). The need for research on the wellness industry's impact on health decisions. *American Journal of Preventive Medicine, 67*(4), 627–630. https://doi.org/10.1016/j.amepre.2024.05.010

American College of Sports Medicine. (2024). **2025 ACSM worldwide fitness trends**. *ACSM's Health & Fitness Journal.* https://journals.lww.com/acsm-healthfitness/fulltext/2024/11000/2025_acsm_worldwide_fitness_trends__future.6.aspx

Budler, M., & Božič, K. (2024). Adopting transitional business models in small fitness businesses in response to business disruptions. *Journal of Small Business Strategy, 33*(3), 92–156. https://doi.org/10.53703/001c.92989

Callaghan, S., Lösch, M., Pione, A., & Teichner, W. (2021). **Feeling good: The future of the US$1.5 trillion wellness market**. McKinsey & Company. https://www.mckinsey.com/~/media/mckinsey/industries/consumer%20packaged%20goods/our%20insights/feeling%20good%20the%20future%20of%20the%201%205%20trillion%20wellness%20market/feelinggoodthefutureofthe15trilliondollarwellnessmarket.pdf

Chekhovska, L. (2017). Fitness industry: State and prospects of development in the countries of the world. *Slobozhanskyi Herald of Science and Sport, 58*(2), 107–112. https://doi.org/10.15391/snsv.2017-2.019

Galante, J., Friedrich, C., Dawson, A. F., Modrego-Alarcón, M., Gebbing, P., Delgado-Suárez, I., Gupta, R., Dean, L., Dalgleish, T., White, I. R., & Jones, P. B. (2021). Mindfulness-based programmes for mental health promotion in adults in nonclinical settings: A systematic review and meta-analysis of randomized controlled trials. *PLOS Medicine, 18*(1), e1003481. https://doi.org/10.1371/journal.pmed.1003481

Global Wellness Institute. (2024, November 5). **The global wellness economy reaches a new peak of US$6.3 trillion and is forecast to hit US$9 trillion by 2028**. https://globalwellnessinstitute.org/press-room/press-releases/the-global-wellness-economy-reaches-a-new-peak-of-6-3-trillion-and-is-forecast-to-hit-9-trillion-by-2028/

M. Dakić, *When Fitness Goes Tech*, https://doi.org/10.1007/979-8-8688-2457-9

Global Wellness Institute. (2025, March 4). **New research shows the U.S. wellness economy – valued at US$2 trillion – now represents one-third of the global wellness economy**. https://globalwellnessinstitute.org/press-room/press-releases/gow-us-econ-valued-at-2trillion/

Grand View Research. (2024). **Fitness app market size, share & trends analysis report, 2024–2030**. https://www.grandviewresearch.com/industry-analysis/fitness-app-market

Grand View Research. (2024). **Smart fitness market size, share & trends analysis report, 2024–2030**. https://www.grandviewresearch.com/industry-analysis/smart-fitness-devices-market

Guo, J., & Fussell, S. R. (2022). "It's great to exercise together on Zoom!": Understanding the practices and challenges of livestream group fitness classes. *Proceedings of the ACM on Human-Computer Interaction, 6*(CSCW1), 1–28. https://doi.org/10.1145/3512918

Kang, H. S., & Exworthy, M. (2022). Wearing the future-Wearables to empower users to take greater responsibility for their health and care: A scoping review. *JMIR mHealth and uHealth, 10*(7), e35684. https://doi.org/10.2196/35684

Les Mills International. (2023). **Gen Z fitness: Cracking the code**. https://www.lesmills.com.au/clubs-and-facilities/gen-fit-training/

Macintosh, E., & Doherty, A. (2007). Reframing the service environment in the fitness industry. *Managing Leisure, 12*(4), 273–289. https://doi.org/10.1080/13606710701546835

McAvoy, C. R., Batrakoulis, A., Camhi, S. M., et al. (2025). **2026 ACSM worldwide fitness trends: Future directions of the health and fitness industry**. *ACSM's Health & Fitness Journal.*

McKinsey & Company. (2024). **Top wellness trends in 2024**. https://www.mckinsey.com/industries/consumer-packaged-goods/our-insights/the-trends-defining-the-1-point-8-trillion-dollar-global-wellness-market-in-2024

McKinsey & Company. (2025). **Future of wellness trends survey**. https://www.mckinsey.com/industries/consumer-packaged-goods/our-insights/future-of-wellness-trends

National Academies of Sciences, Engineering, and Medicine. (2022). *Challenges and opportunities for precision and personalized nutrition: Proceedings of a workshop.* National Academies Press. https://doi.org/10.17226/26299

Statista. (2024). **Fitness apps worldwide – market outlook**. https://www.statista.com/outlook/hmo/digital-health/digital-fitness-well-being/health-wellness-coaching/fitness-apps/worldwide

Warby Parker & Google. (2025, December 8). *Warby Parker, Google to launch AI-powered smart glasses in 2026*. Reuters. https://www.reuters.com/business/warby-parker-google-launch-ai-powered-smart-glasses-2026-2025-12-08/

U.S. Bureau of Labor Statistics. (2024). **Fitness trainers and instructors**. *Occupational Outlook Handbook*. https://www.bls.gov/ooh/personal-care-and-service/fitness-trainers-and-instructors.htm

Index

A

AI, *see* Artificial intelligence (AI)
AI-powered apps, 180
AI-powered fitness studio management, 152
AI-powered studio management, 152, 153, 155
AI-powered wearables, 148
American College of Sports Medicine (ACSM), 108
AR, *see* Augmented reality (AR)
Artificial intelligence (AI), xvii, 3, 5, 25
Artificial intelligence (AI), fitness
- applications, 147, 148
- business management, 148
- categories, 146
- challenges and limitations, 149–151
- data-driven approaches, 145
- immersive fitness experiences, 148
- software examples
  - fitness owners, 158–160
  - fitness users, 156, 158
- studio management, 152, 153, 155

Augmented reality (AR), 3, 19, 34, 166

B

Biohacking, 28, 35
Biometric analysis, 148, 160
Biometric sync, 19

C

CAGR, *see* Compound annual growth rate (CAGR)
ChatGPT, 39
Compound annual growth rate (CAGR), xix, 30
CRM, *see* Customer relationship management (CRM)
Customer relationship management (CRM), 59, 69, 102

E

eSports, 25
E-textiles, 123
Experience economy, 29, 35

F

Fitbod, 18
Fitness
- apps, 178–180
  - posture/form and motion tracking, 183, 184
  - recovery and stress, 182
- clubs, xxi

Fitness sector
- AI-driven social motivation, 168
- digital transformation challenges, 7
  - adoption barriers, 7
  - business model disruption, 8

M. Dakić, *When Fitness Goes Tech*, https://doi.org/10.1007/979-8-8688-2457-9

Fitness sector (*cont.*)
data privacy and security concerns, 8
personalization limitations, 9
ROI difficulties, 9–11
technical and operational issues, 9
technology integration, 7
digital transformation, opportunities
AI personalization, 5, 6
community, 5
consumers' habits, 3
global reach, 4
health habits, 2
hybrid fitness experience, 4
revenue streams/market dynamcs, 5
technology innovations, 3, 4
digitization, 1, 2
eco-smart fitness, 168
holistic health ecosystems, 167
personalization, 165
personalized and holistic experiences, 170
predictive healthcare, 166
smart fitness equipment and gyms, 167
trends evolution, 13, 15
Fitness technology
adopters, 37
client or user, 42, 43, 45, 46
professional, 40–42
virtual classes and loyalty programs, 37
FitOn, 18
Freeletics, 18

G

General Data Protection Regulation (GDPR), 57
Glofox (ABC Glofox), 69, 95
GMS, *see* Gym management software (GMS); Gym management system (GMS)
Google Glass, 121
Gym management software (GMS), xviii, xix, 35, 171–174
Gym management system (GMS), 31
advanced analytics, 51
alternatives, 66
benefits, 67, 68
business, 62, 63
business mobile applications, 47
class-centered platforms, 77–79
client app, benefits, 85, 86
complete fitness solutions, 68–73
custom *vs.* ready-made, 65, 66
digital ecosystem, 47, 48
digital solution, 50
features
attendance/access control, 57, 58
billing and payment processing, 59
CRM module, 59
marketing and engagement tools, 61
membership management, 57
POS system, 61
reporting and analytics, 59
scheduling and class management, 58
staff and member app, 57
staff and payroll management, 60
limitations, 54–56
marketing campaigns, 51
Niche fitness, 73–77
security, 64, 65
staff and owners, 50

staff app, benefits, 85
staff app *vs.* client app, 81–84
user journeys, 52, 54
Gym management tools, 37
GymMaster, 95

H

Health apps/mobile and web
AR, 130
community-driven fitness platforms, 130
educational and skill-learning fitness software, 130
holistic and AI coaching apps, 131
interactive and smart training software, 129
live-stream/virtual group workouts, 128
meditation/wellness apps, 127
nutrition apps, 127, 128
personal/online coaching, 129
recovery/sleep/wellness app, 131
training/coaching/AI, 125–127
video-based platforms, 128
Hexoskin, 22
Hybrid fitness solutions, 117, 143
bonus, 124
E-textiles, 123
smart home-gym equipment, 122, 123
wearable technology, 118–121
Hybrid technology trends
AR/VR and metaverse, 19–21
gamification, 24
holistic health, 24
smart gym equipment, 22, 23
smart gyms, 17–19
wearable technology, 16
Hyper-personalized fitness ecosystems, 169

I, J

Internet of Things (IoT), 3

K, L

Key performance indicators (KPIs), 51, 59

M

Machine learning (ML), 38, 146, 152, 161
Microsoft HoloLens, 121
Mindbody, 95
Mindbody user app, 69
ML, *see* Machine learning (ML)
Myx Fitness, 18
Myzone, 18

N

Nike Training Club, 18, 27
Nutrigenomics, 29

O

Online fitness, xx, 105–107
Online stores, 52
OxeFit, 23

P, Q

Peloton, 18
Personal trainer (PT)
fitness instructor, 87
monetization model, 98

Personal trainer (PT) (*cont.*)
factors, 98–100
fitness consumers, 100, 101
fitness leaders, 102
platforms, 90–97
Personal training (PT) software, 103
benefits, 89, 90
coaches and personal trainers, 87
features, 88
Point-of-sale (POS), 52, 61, 102
Prana Wearable, 22
PT, *see* Personal trainer (PT)

R

RhinoFit, 95

S

Small to medium-sized businesses (SMBs), 49
Smart machines/home gyms, 181
Smartwatches, 109, 112, 119, 120
Software-based fitness solutions, 143
Software fitness solutions
AR/VR, 116
community support, 117
educational and skill-learning, 116
interactive training software, 115, 116
live-stream classes, 115
mobile and web apps, 112, 113
personal and online coaching, 115
physical devices, 112
video-based fitness platforms, 114
virtual group workouts, 115
Software technology trends
AI powered applications, 25–27
biometric tracking, 28, 29
experience economy, 29
GMS, 30, 31
live streaming classes, 32, 33
staff and client management apps, 33
Web3 technologies, 31, 32
Speediance, 23
Strava, 18
Strava MyFitnessPal, 27
Subscription-based model, 76

T, U

TeamUp pricing model, 72
Technology trends, 143
fitness enthusiasts, quiz, 138–142
fitness mobile/web apps, 109, 110
smart fitness machines, 110
virtual and on-demand fitness classes, 110
VR/AR fitness, 111
wearable technology, 109
Tempo, 18
Tonal, 23

V

Video-based fitness platforms, 114
Virtuagym, 95
Virtual reality (VR), 3, 19, 34, 166
VR, *see* Virtual reality (VR)

W, X, Y, Z

Wearable fitness trackers
Activinsights Ltd., 136
Amazfit Active Smartwatch, 135
Ambiotex GmbH, 135
Apple, Inc., 132

Fitbit, Inc., 133
Gabit, 134
Gamin ltd., 132
Google, 137
Huawei Technologies Co. Ltd., 133
meta and ray-ban smart glasses, 137
Oura Ring, 136
Polar Electro Oy, 134
Samsung Electronics Co. Ltd., 133
Sensoria Inc., 135
ultrahuman ring, 137
Vuzix/RealWear, 138
Whoop.Inc., 136
Xiaomi corporation, 134
Wearable/health trackers
chest straps and arm monitor, 176
fitness bands, 176
medical and advanced health trackers, 177
smart apparel/smart fabric, 178
smart rings, 177
smartwatches, 175
Wearable technology, 16, 34, 118
Web3 technologies, 31, 35